New Year 1985 - 86.

A Tournier Companion

A Tournier Companion

SCM PRESS LTD

334 01664 9

First published 1976
by SCM Press Ltd
58 Bloomsbury Street London WC1

Filmset by Filmtype Services Limited, Scarborough
and printed in Great Britain by
Billing & Sons Limited
London, Guildford & Worcester

Contents

Introducing Paul Tournier

Paul Tournier is the son of Louis Tournier, a staunch Calvinist and well-known preacher and teacher, at one time pastor of the Cathedral of St Peter in Geneva. Paul was born in 1898, eight years after his father's marriage to his second wife Elizabeth Ormond, a girl who had been his student. Three months after his son's birth Louis died, to be followed six years later by his wife, whose brother took the orphaned Paul and his sister Louise into his home and brought them up.

Paul had already decided by the age of twelve that he wanted to be a doctor, and although his school career was not distinguished he soon proved to be an outstanding medical student at the university in Geneva. He was also a popular leader among his contemporaries, and was elected President of the Zofingia, a country-wide student body. During his time at university, he helped the International Red Cross after the First World War in their work of repatriating Russian and Austrian Prisoners of War, and in that connection travelled widely in Eastern Europe.

After graduating from the university in 1923, Paul Tournier spent one year as a junior doctor in Paris, before returning to Geneva to spend a further four years at the Polytechnic. Then, in 1928, he entered private practice in Geneva, and remained in it until his recent retirement. For the whole of his career, Paul Tournier was a General Practitioner. He had no specialist training in psychiatry, and has never called himself a psychiatrist.

Such is the simple outline of Paul Tournier's career. Yet at a very deep level, his own experiences, both as a child and as an adult, shaped his life and outlook; and his own development as a person dictated the direction of his work.

The death of his father while he was a baby drew the child Paul very close to his mother, and her death when he was only six consequently had a very profound effect on him. The aunt who brought him up, although kind, was a rather unstable character, which further increased the child's loneliness and confusion. He used to retreat into solitude and fantasy, and of course became very shy. His own early decision to become a doctor was partly made as a result of his mother's long illness and death and partly because his uncle was careful to keep alive in him the image of his pastor father. Although it would not be in exactly the same way, he, too, decided to care for people.

Paul Tournier's university career and early years as a junior doctor began for him the process of his own escape from loneliness and shyness. Shortly afterwards, however, he underwent an experience which shaped the whole course of his future life. Although as the son of a Calvinist pastor he could hardly have escaped religious influence, his own religion at that time was rather the intellectual support of an ideal than a living faith. In 1932, when he was thirty-four, Tournier met in Geneva some members of a new religious movement, the Oxford Group. The significant features of their experience were the surrender of one's life to Christ; guidance through quiet reflection and meditation; the practice of Christian moral virtues; and sharing in group fellowship. Tournier talked with members of this group, who shared with him their experience of meditation. Gradually, through practice, he himself learnt its value, and he came to relax in the awareness of God and grow to knowledge of himself as a person, and of God as a real, living presence in his own life. This discovery of a personal, vital religion had a deep effect on Tournier's life and work. It led him into the inquiry of personality, and to the practice of what he called the 'medicine of the person'. By 1937 he felt so strongly that his work would be taking a new direction that he wrote to all his patients to tell them of it. He explained that he would be going beyond the treatment of physical complaints to the deep problems within the personality of the patient. His aim would be to restore harmony and unity to the whole person by the practice of medical knowledge combined with psychological understanding and religious experience. Tournier's first book, *The Healing of Persons* (now out of print in Britain), written soon after that letter of 1937, is an attempt to work out his method of practice in the light of his own spiritual renewal. His own maturity, of course, was essential to the approach he adopted of entering into close, personal relationships with his patients. He has always maintained the habit of daily reflection, meditation and personal commitment.

In the late 1930s the Oxford Group, which had led Tournier into this path, began to change its own direction and occupy itself with social and political action. In 1938 it grew into the Moral Rearmament movement (MRA) and not long afterwards, Tournier made the difficult decision to sever his connections. However, the group had also taught Tournier the value of fellowship and sharing, and in 1947 he was instrumental in bringing another group into being. With two other doctors (both still members of the original group) he organized a meeting of doctors who had as their common purpose the concern to cultivate the medicine of the person. The new group met at the Château de Bossey, near Geneva, and was therefore known as the Bossey Group. So that the group should have some specific direction, after the initial meetings Tournier himself prepared some studies based on the biblical basis of medicine. *A Doctor's Casebook in the Light of the Bible* grew out of some of these papers. Tournier still attends the annual meetings of the group, though he no longer has any responsiblity for its organization.

How Tournier has developed and practised his work will be evident to readers of this *Companion*. The problems of loneliness and fear which he felt as a small boy, the frustrations of people needing a place and vocation and the special problems of old age are all encompassed in his life and experience, and find expression in the writing which he has continued throughout his career and into retirement. The typescripts which he sends to his publishers are meticulously written out in his own neat hand. Translations of the books are too numerous to list, but it is one of Dr Tournier's favourite hobbies to keep track of all the various printings in each language, and to compile statistics of the total number of copies in circulation. *A Doctor's Casebook in the Light of the Bible*, for instance, has been translated from its original French into English, German, Finnish, Japanese, Dutch, Swedish, Spanish, Norwegian and Italian, and a total of thirty-nine publishers have more than one and three-quarter million of Paul Tournier's books in print in sixteen languages. Until her death a few years ago Madame Tournier was a constant encouragement and companion to him in his life and the various aspects of his work; but although he no longer has her support, he is still very active in retirement and is even now busily engaged in writing another book – on violence.

Beginning

All life is an adventure, and all adventure has its difficulties. The path of life is always strewn with failures. What complicates the problem still further is that life's successes are as dangerous as its failures. 'I fear success more than anything,' wrote Bernard Shaw. 'To have succeeded means that one has finished one's work on this earth. . . . Life has meaning for me only if it remains a perpetual becoming, a definite goal in front of one and not behind.' This is the paradoxical law of adventure, namely, that the thing that puts an end to it is its success. Success is perilous.

(*The Adventure of Living,* 140)

It is impossible to overdo the cultivation of a liking for adventure in children. Baden-Powell understood this fact well when he made the lure of adventure the chief educative motive in the Scout movement. But an observation should be made at this point. Some people remain Scouts all their lives. They take pleasure in wearing the juvenile uniform complete with its mysterious decorations. It is not difficult to see that they also retain an infantile personality; in some way they have become fixed at a stage of youthful adventure. They have not accepted the law of adventure, which is that it must die in order to be born again. It is in fact through the continual dying of even our most exciting adventures that we reach maturity. In this way we are made available for other adventures, adventures which will be less infantile and naïve, more adult and fruitful.

Many people are never able to come to terms with the death to which every adventure is inevitably subject. We see them everywhere in search of some stimulant, some new and life-giving current that will relight the torch of their passion. Their lives are a succession of wild enthusiasms for one idea after another, no matter what. But the very versatility of their advocacy largely detracts from its effectiveness. Rather are they a liability to the various causes they claim to serve, since in reality these are only being used as a means of satisfying their own need to be active.

(*The Adventure of Living,* 21)

The liveliness of the child comes of his not yet having, like the adult, been subjected to the inexorable mould of automatism. His spontaneity is contagious: he makes us feel freer, as if the too close-fitting garment which was constricting us has been loosened. And when a man becomes set in a rigid mode of thought and habit, we feel that he has grown prematurely old, that life is being extinguished in him. He always repeats the same formulae of word and action. His reaction to every situation can be foreseen. He is nothing more than a well-trained animal.

Indeed, it is not what is really human, but the merely animal in us that is automatic. This is incontestably the case with the all-powerful working of our instincts; it is also true of the conditioned reflexes implanted in us by education and habit.

(*The Meaning of Persons,* 97)

Conscious of the greatness of God – beyond the measure of our minds – and of the power of sin which dulls our perception, the true believer seeks his road step by step, combining faith with the most realistic self-criticism. He is always on the lookout for some sign sent from God to confirm his faith, or else to correct some error in it.

Jesus himself spent years at the workbench before assuming his mission. He himself told of his inner struggles in the desert and in Gethsemane. He went every morning to seek God's commands in prayer.

St Paul, that giant in the faith, spent fourteen years meditating in the desert after his conversion. And in the case of so many others – St Francis of Assisi, St Bernard, Pascal, Luther, and our own Vinet – what struggles, what gropings in the dark, what a sense of the mysteries of God and the powerlessness of man fully to know him in this world!

We recognize the spiritual authority of these men in this very sincerity. That is why we believe them to have come nearer the truth than others, because it commanded their assent through myriad doubts. That is why the suggestions that come to us from them, all wonderfully consistent, seem to us more worthy of credence than those of many others who are much surer of themselves in what they hold as truth.

(*The Person Reborn,* 161f.)

Our trouble is that we are less certain of God's will than Jesus Christ was. And the danger of being mistaken is always greatest at the moment when we flatter ourselves that we know his will. At that point we are already falling into the error of magic, claiming to penetrate the secrets of God. But without ever being sure that we know in advance that God requires of us, we may never stop humbly seeking his will. This is the first necessity in the exercise of our vocation.

(*A Doctor's Casebook,* 117)

I often think that the best things we do in this life are done without our intending to do them. I am on a journey, and let an old friend know that I am going to drop in and see him. When I get there he tells me of the great and wonderful experience he has had on confessing to his wife a fault he has been hiding from her for a long time. For a long time, too, he has felt called to make this confession, but has not had the courage to do so. The announcement of my visit sufficed to make him do it. And he thanks me warmly for the help I have given him in this way, and for which I can claim no merit at all!

In the same way our moments of greatest happiness often come quite unexpectedly, and if we tried to hold on to them or reproduce them, it would be in vain.

(*The Person Reborn,* 85)

Sometimes a man realizes that his occupation does not fit in with his ambitions, that in fact when he made his choice he had not the courage to take the risks he knew he was called to take. In such a case the rebirth of the person may have to be paid for by a heavy sacrifice of material security. Such an honest choice, however late it comes, is as fruitful as the 'provisional' life is sterile, dragging on from one employment to another with no whole-hearted commitment of the self to any of them. Having a vocation means acting in a spirit of vocation, being convinced that what one is doing is what one is called to do.

But the trouble is that in practice it is not easy to choose between these two roads – between abandoning resolutely one's present life in order to make the life of one's dreams come true, and renouncing the dream in order to throw oneself wholeheartedly into one's present situation. Worst of all is to be unwilling to give up either of them. It is better to make a mistake in an honest choice than never to choose at all.

(*The Meaning of Persons,* 207f.)

It is not a question of excelling, but of 'having a go'. Do not say that such and such an activity does not interest you before you have tried it. Everything becomes interesting if one is prepared to stick at it for a while. You will find that it is trying it out that counts.

(*Learning to Grow Old,* 107)

There is no human decision that does not spring from an intimate mixture of both good and bad motives. It is impossible ever to disentangle them entirely. And even from a flight, a mistake, an illusion, and even more, from a fault, an act of disobedience, a sin, God can produce good. *Felix culpa!*

So even if a vocation has been taken up to some extent from wrong motives, it can be genuine and fruitful. Faith consists, in fact, in seeing the hand of God in it, and in following it in a spirit of service towards him.

(*The Person Reborn,* 79f.)

Know yourself!

Man has always been incomprehensible to himself, but he is more tragically conscious of it today than in the last century. The discoveries of psychoanalysis have revealed to him that there is in the depth of his soul a secret closet whose key he has lost. What is there in this closet of the unconscious? What feelings, what desires, what emotions, what memories, what impulses, what hopes, what remorse? He can only perceive a few colourless traces, a few troubling and uncertain reflections. There is a mysterious inner secret down there which is frightening. The more progress a man makes in self-analysis, the more he realizes what is still missing and will always be missing in the discovery of himself.

I believe that it is one of the principal causes of the anguish which characterizes man of today and which the existentialists have also made us feel. He indeed knows that he is always more or less on stage, that he strives to seem what he wants to seem in order to hide better what he is, but he does not know what he is hiding or what it is. He indeed knows that no matter how beautiful his life may be, it is only a fresco that he has painted on the door of his secret closet. That is exactly what Jesus Christ was describing, long ago, when he spoke of 'whited sepulchres' (Matthew 23.27). But what is there then in this sepulchre where all the repressed rubbish of all humanity as well as of our own past is rotting?

(*Secrets,* 44f.)

Introspection does not throw any sure light on oneself: 'I am thirty-six, and I do not know yet whether I am miserly or prodigal, sober or gluttonous.' These words from the pen of André Gide are tragic. Moreover, introspection actually alters the person. Paul Claudel writes: 'Merely by looking at ourselves we falsify ourselves.' Self-examination is an exhausting undertaking. The mind becomes so engrossed in it that it loses its normal capacity for relationship with the world and with God. Locked in a narrow round of endless and sterile self-analysis, the person becomes shrunk and deformed, while false problems multiply *ad infinitum*.

That shrewd judge of human nature, Saint Francis de Sales, had already written: 'It is not possible that the Spirit of God should dwell in a mind that wishes to know too much of what is happening within itself. . . . You are afraid of being afraid, then you are afraid of being afraid of being afraid. Some vexation vexes you, and then you are vexed at being vexed by that vexation. In the same way I have often seen people who, having lost their tempers, are afterwards angry at having been angry. All this is like the circles made when a stone is cast into the water – first a little circle forms, and that in its turn makes a bigger one, and that one makes yet another.'

(*The Meaning of Persons*, 68f.)

I do not say that delving into ourselves is entirely valueless; it opens up a rich field for discovery; the trouble is that it is too rich. Every time we are sincere about it we see that some attitude which we thought we had taken up spontaneously is in fact the result of mechanisms which, because they are more deep-seated, we take to be more authentically personal. An experience of that sort is always moving and humbling, as well as fruitful. We have the impression, or rather the overwhelming conviction, that we are seeing ourselves to be quite different from what we supposed. But it is an exploration which can go on for ever. If our sincerity is exacting, we soon see that we have doffed our garment only to find another beneath it.

In fact, what in the blinding light of the discovery we have taken to be our true person, is still only an aspect of it – a real one, certainly, but incomplete. On analysis it proves once more to be determined by deeper mechanisms. And so we could go on, until we reached the unconscious forces which are no longer personal at all: the impulsions of instinct, noted by Freud, which we possess in common with the animals, or the ancestral archetypes of the collective unconscious, described by Jung, which we have in common with all other human beings. We should then be in the presence only of completely impersonal forces of nature.

Thus, the result of our quest is that the person, through having its successive envelopes peeled off one by one, vanishes in our hands. One can understand, then, Shri Ramakrishna's remark: 'Think well, and you will see that there is nothing you can call "I". As you peel an onion, there is always another layer, but you never reach the kernel. So when you analyse the ego, it disappears completely.'

(*The Meaning of Persons*, 71)

Very few people judge themselves fairly. Some are too sure of themselves, a rather disagreeable trait which marks them out as of mediocre personality. But others – more sensitive, more adult and more agreeable – easily fall into a sort of prejudice against themselves. The striking thing is the complete hopelessness of any attempt to bring them to a more objective view. It is no use pointing out all their good qualities. They look upon it as cruel irony, so clear does it seem to them that we are speaking of the very qualities they lack! For our part, we feel that this systematic negation of their obvious qualities is like an insatiable quest for compliments which, however, never reassure them.

A pretty woman has doubts about her own beauty and thinks she sees scorn in the insistent glances of the men who are attracted by her good looks. A man of modest gifts, who is nevertheless self-confident, knows instinctively how to make the most of the few talents he has at his disposal. Another, richly endowed with talent, stakes everything on other qualities which he would like to, but does not, possess. Or if he does happen to discover some authentic capacity in himself, he is so afraid of not making anything of it that he makes a blunder and suffers all the more from his failure because it is undeserved. Failures in such circumstances can have incalculable consequences on a person's whole life.

One can but deplore the injustice of fate which gives a much greater reward to the audacity, the clever manoeuvre, even the bluff of some than to the real value of others. And society is very much the loser for it! Think of the countless people whose valuable talents remain for ever hidden, sterilized, because they did not receive the necessary encouragement at the right moment. It is the best who are most unsure of themselves! I am always taken aback by this. Just because they are more keenly aware of what is at stake in life, because they have higher ideals of perfection and service, they are obsessed by how far they always fall short of the realization of their dreams, as well as of ours.

(*The Adventure of Living,* 112)

I cannot keep count of the number of people in whom religion, the love of God and the desire to serve him, or even a quite secular ideal of perfection, lead only to a life of sterility, sadness and anxiety. The fear of sinning has killed all their spontaneity. The subtle analysis of their consciences has taken the place of that childlike simplicity of heart which Christ demands. All joy has been replaced by the pursuit of duty. They have come to the point of doing nothing that gives them pleasure, as if God, who loves us, never required any but disagreeable things of us! They make incredible efforts, but win no victories. They are always comparing themselves with those they look upon as their betters.

(*The Person Reborn,* 82)

Our human condition can never escape from a tension between irreconcilable aspirations. We cannot give way to them both at once; we can only give free play first to one and then to the other – if possible at the right moment! Yes, at the right moment: that is why problems of conduct are not so much questions of principle, that can be settled once and for all, as practical questions the answers to which depend on the circumstances of the time. Voltaire said that there were four ways of wasting one's time: doing nothing, not doing what one ought, doing it badly, and doing it at the wrong moment. A musician cannot play a *do* without first silencing the *re*, the *mi*, and all the other notes; he cannot play other notes without silencing the *do*, on pain of producing, not a harmony, but a frightful cacophony. Making music means playing each note at the right moment.

We can never satisfy all our instinctive or moral impulses at the same time. There is no life without repression. We cannot be generous without repressing our egoism, or give way to egoism without repressing our generosity. We cannot give free rein to our fancy except by repressing our need for order, or give way to our need for order without clipping the wings of our fancy. A woman said to me the other day, 'There is both a nun and a bohemian in me. I've tried in vain all my life to reconcile them.' We cannot boldly commit ourselves without repressing our fears, or succumb to fear without experiencing a longing to be bold.

Only the animals are fully spontaneous, living unmixed the feelings of the fleeting moment. The child, too, surprises us with his capacity to go rapidly from disappointment to joy. But in the adult there is no laughter that does not hide secret tears, either unadmitted or unconscious, nor are there any tears behind which is not some repressed enjoyment. There is no self-giving without some reticence, no withholding without some longing to give.

(*The Adventure of Living*, 159f.)

Psychological analysis reveals that much that is good and valuable, many noble acts and generous efforts, are in reality compensations for those same secret anxieties which overwhelm the weak. They are not for that reason to be despised; but it is useful to be aware of this compensatory mechanism if one wishes to know oneself and to understand others.

I realize now how much my own intellectual activity was stimulated by unconscious complexes when I was a student. Though I never admitted it to myself I was terribly lonely; I was afraid of other people. Then I perceived that my aptitude for handling, formulating and defending ideas could be used as an admission-ticket to society. I could thus win the affection and esteem for which I craved in order to bolster up my self-confidence. I played the card. I wrote plays, I mugged up mathematics, studied law, made long speeches, became president of my students' union, threw myself into work for the Red Cross and then for the Church, and passed my medical examinations with flying colours.

None of this delivered me from my secret complex, but it

helped me to hide it. In my heart, compromise and defeat still went on, but at least I was able to some extent to forget them. I do not now repudiate those youthful enthusiasms, nor the intellectual and religious truths for which I fought. Later on I underwent spiritual crises, in which I felt how much there was of artificiality in the zeal with which I used to defend doctrines too often belied by my real life. The discovery, far from undermining my convictions, fortified and renewed them, requiring of me more conformity between theory and practice.

(*The Strong and the Weak*, 131)

A person's attitude at any given moment has a large number of meanings at once. A patient breaks away from his family background. It is perhaps pride which impels him to do so. Or perhaps it is a defensive reaction against the authoritarianism of his father; or maybe he is doing so in compensation for an inner disquiet. Lastly, he may be responding to a real call to break out of the debilitating comfort of his life and face up to the adventure of life. His decision may have many more meanings besides, and all of them may be true at once. I understood this when the psychoanalysts taught me that a dream was always susceptible of various interpretations, all of them true. It is our intellectualism which keeps on asking which is the true one. All of them contain something of the truth, and each enriches our vision of reality. The moment I think I have understood the cause of a given piece of behaviour, I have closed my mind to the possibility of research on other aspects of the behaviour. The moment I think I have understood someone, I stop helping him, because I am no longer in an attitude of seeking. Man is an inexhaustible mystery. He fits into none of our categories of thought.

(*The Person Reborn*, 107)

Every grace has its dangers, and not only for others. Who would dare deny that there is a considerable amount of pride in the sense of well-being and exaltation felt by the person who bears witness to the fine spiritual experiences that have been granted to him? I once took it into my head to reform my handwriting, since my hasty scribble, although it saved me time, wasted that of my readers; it was a sign of lack of love. But recently I caught myself contemplating my writing with an improper self-love, and taking particular care with it in order to give a good impression!

I have met many nurses and social workers who were in conflict with their families. Their pride in having chosen a career of social service made them adopt at home a condescending attitude towards their brothers and sisters which set the whole family against them.

'God is the creative fire,' one of my patients once wrote, 'and the devil is the destructive fire!'

But just try to separate the destructive from the creative fire! It is all according to the use one makes of it. That same flame which is at the basis of the whole of civilization can, if we are not careful, start the most terrible conflagrations.

(*The Person Reborn*, 78)

One man always acts with impeccable correctness, but only with great difficulty does he admit to me what his behaviour is like in secret. Another always appears extremely serious-minded, but has childish habits which he carefully hides. A devoutly religious man lays bare to me the intolerable tragedy of his life: he is generally thought of as an example of serene piety, whereas in reality he is haunted constantly by sexual obsessions.

How many people there are who are one thing at home and something quite different outside! In their homes they have themselves waited on like Eastern potentates; outside they live lives of devotion to others. Authoritarian, tyrannical and argumentative at home; patient and conciliatory in the outside world. Silent and unapproachable at home; chatty and companionable outside. A pastor whose ministry is full of life and much appreciated, confesses himself incapable of praying alone with his wife. In all our hearts, faith is mixed with doubt, love with bitterness. I have dealt here with the contradictions of the human heart only from the psychological standpoint. I have not touched on the moral conflict, which St Paul describes in the Epistle to the Romans: 'For the good that I would I do not: but the evil which I would not, that I do' (7.19).

It is extremely difficult for us to acknowledge this utterly illogical and contradictory character of our feelings.

(*The Meaning of Persons,* 53f.)

A lack of knowledge of psychology can harm the religious life. It is well known that the law of the association of ideas is such that any thought, however outrageous or shocking, may at any moment cross our minds, as a result of an association with some quite ordinary idea. These associations form as it were a kaleidoscopic film ceaselessly running through the back of our minds. We scarcely notice them, so swiftly do they chase one another across our consciousness, unless we pay particular attention to them or take particular pleasure in them. There is no question of moral responsibility being involved in this automatic process of association of ideas. A sincere believer, however, lacking proper instruction in the matter and clinging to the ideal of moral perfection, is shocked to find an improper and vulgar thought coming into his mind. The effect of this is to concentrate his attention upon the intruding thought – 'stopping the film at that point'. And so the whole religious life of the patient is thereafter concentrated upon an unreal problem arising from a confusion between free association and temptation, as well as between temptation and sin. The more lacking in true moral content the problem is, the greater is the tendency for it to become obsessive.

(*The Person Reborn,* 16f.)

We are not only one personage throughout our lives; we are innumerable personages. At each new encounter we show ourselves different; with one friend we are the serious thinker; with another, the wag; we change our demeanour to suit each new situation. We are even many personages at once.

There is in me the troubled and anxious man, full of doubts about myself and about everything else, who himself knows all the anxieties and all the failures that my patients come to confess to me. There is in me the steadfast believer, who has had solid experience of God's grace, and who witnesses to it with conviction. In me there is one who wishes to parade even this honest desire. There is in me the doctor who believes passionately in his medicine, and eagerly runs to help his fellowmen; there is in me the egoist and sceptic, who would like to run away and hide in a solitary cabin.

(*The Meaning of Persons*, 73)

It is the common experience of all, that humanity moves between the two poles of simplicity and complexity. People who have the sort of mind that sees only one side to every question tend towards vigorous action. They succeed in everything they do because they do not stop to split hairs and have abounding confidence in their own abilities. Your successful journalist, for instance, is inclined to simplify every problem and condense it into an arresting phrase. On the other hand, those with subtle and cultivated minds tend to get lost in a maze of fine distinctions. They always see how complicated things really are, so that their powers of persuasion are nil. That is why the world is led by those who are least suited to raising its cultural and moral standards. It is only very few who manage to combine both tendencies, and in my view a lively Christian faith is the best precondition for the accomplishment of this miracle, because it gives both profound understanding and simplicity of heart.

(*The Person Reborn*, 20f.)

We all have our fads and our failings. As the proverb says, no man is a hero to his valet. We all have our bees in our bonnets, our habits which we can no longer forsake, and that is not a little humiliating. Sometimes they are costly: how many husbands are there who are careful not to tell their wives how much they earn, in order to be able to hide from them (perhaps to hide from themselves) exactly what they spend on mediocre pleasures, while at the same time they exhort their wives to economize with the housekeeping money. And the wives often put down as 'groceries' the expensive beauty-products they are unable to resist the temptation to buy.

So we are all afraid of reality; we pretend to want to know

ourselves, and we are afraid of knowing ourselves. Even when we consult them, we are always a little frightened of the graphologist, the psychotechnician or the psychiatrist. It is not only the picture that other people have of us that we are afraid of having to revise, but also the picture that we ourselves have of other people. For the young and adventurous frame of mind which is ready and eager to discover ourselves as well as others, we soon substitute the fatal pretension of knowing ourselves and knowing our neighbours.

(*The Meaning of Persons*, 151f.)

Fear

No endeavour is fruitful without fear. There is no good actor who does not have to contend with stage-fright. There is no lecturer listened to who does not tremble. Desire, fear and sorrow, as St Augustine pointed out, may come from the love of good and of charity; they are not in themselves vices. 'Fear,' wrote Dubois, 'within certain limits, is an eminently useful emotion.'

To reject the utopian idea of a life without fear, to accept our human condition, fear-ridden as it is, this is not merely resignation. It is to accept fear as a blessing from God, with its part to play in his purpose for mankind.

Fear is universal because it is an instinct; it is the instrument of the instinct of self-preservation. It has a providential significance. It is the source of all progress. It is the motive force of the whole of civilization; that of science, which seeks to pierce the terrifying mysteries of nature; that of philosophy and religion, whose quest is truth; that of labour, of agriculture and industry, by which men strive against their material insecurity; that of society, of social collaboration, by which they join forces and forget the things that divide them. This is clearly seen when a country threatened by danger from outside realizes the dedicated unity and social peace which has always eluded it in easier times. It is the fear of everything new which gives personal and social life its stability and the framework of habits without which all is confusion. It is also fear which – fortunately! – restrains men from blind obedience of their passions, whose fatal consequences they have learnt from experience.

(*The Strong and the Weak*, 91)

Fear creates what it fears. It is confirmed daily as I observe the behaviour of individuals: stage-fright inhibits speech; the fear of being like one's father or mother leads to an ever-increasing resemblance, and plays a part at least as important as true heredity; the fear of not keeping one's resolutions prevents them being made whole-heartedly, so that failure is inevitable; the fear of succumbing to masturbation makes it certain that one will succumb; the fear of going mad makes us so nervous that those around us assure us that we are heading for madness; the fear of 'cracking', of not having strength enough for a task, saps our strength so that we do 'crack'; the fear of disappointing her fiancé prevents a girl acting naturally, so that she does disappoint him; the fear of not being loved warps a woman's outlook, so that her husband wearies of her and becomes estranged; the fear of not being pretty enough makes her lose her good looks and impels her to disfigure herself with ridiculous make-up; the fear of growing thin stops her putting on weight; the fear of losing his wife's confidence turns a man into a dissembler, so that he arouses her mistrust; the fear of growing old makes us grow prematurely old; the fear of suffering leads us into a thousand errors which bring endless suffering in their train; the fear of penury leads us to speculations in which we lose the little we have; the fear of unemployment makes a young man change his job, so that he finishes up without one; or his fear of not being able to marry, through not having a good enough job, deprives him of the energy he needs to succeed in his career. 'I have come to realize,' a woman told me once, 'that my fear of death was really a fear of dying before I had done what I most wanted to do.' And it was just that fear that was preventing her doing it.

(*The Strong and the Weak*, 69f.)

There is no life without desire; there is no desire without fear; one cannot desire a thing without being afraid of not obtaining it.

We cannot obtain in this world all that we desire. Therefore we cannot live without fear; without the fear of being obstructed from without or from within the accomplishment of our desires – from without by the forces of nature and the will of others, from within by our moral conscience.

(*The Strong and the Weak*, 79)

The fear of not succeeding is, for many people, the biggest obstacle in their way. It holds them back from trying anything at all. And for lack of trying they never give themselves a chance of succeeding – the very thing that would cure them of their doubts. It is not, after all, such a terrible thing not to succeed straight away in some new undertaking. What is serious is to give up, to become stuck in a life that just gets emptier.

(*Learning to Grow Old*, 147f.)

Meeting

Every human being needs secrecy in order to become himself and no longer only a member of his tribe. It is one of the misfortunes of the present day that the living space of every family is more and more restricted: political and military events drive people before them and pile up refugees; building has not caught up with the increase in population; the profit motive is responsible for making apartments even smaller. In these conditions no one any longer has space of his own; parents, brothers and sisters, all live on top of each other, without a secret corner all their own. Every human being needs secrecy in order to collect his thoughts and for others to respect his secrecy. To respect the secrecy of whoever it may be, even your own child, is to respect his individuality. To intrude upon his private life, to violate his secrecy, is to violate his individuality.

(*Secrets*, 22f.)

In the multitudinous contacts of social life, how often do we commit our inmost selves in the apparent dialogue? One can chat endlessly, engage in abstruse intellectual arguments, read whole libraries and so make the acquaintance of all kinds of authors, travel the world over, be a dilettante collector of all sorts of impressions, react like an automaton to every caprice of sentiment, without ever really encountering another person, or discovering oneself by taking up a position with regard to him. Think of the haste and superficiality of modern life, radio programmes flitting from one triviality to another, the 'permanent' cinema, 'Digests' that skim over everything, organized touring that leaves no time for really making contact with things and people.

(*The Meaning of Persons*, 131)

Think of what goes to make up most conversations: the exchange of superficial impressions ('What gorgeous weather!'); conventional remarks that do not always come from the heart ('How are you?'); observations whose true intention is self-justification or more or less cleverly to make the most of oneself; flattery; straightforward or veiled criticism. Here again I must beware of utopianism: it would simply not be human to wish to divest the dialogue of everything superfluous; it would become dry and pedantic, devoid of all graciousness and poetry.

The small-talk of everyday life can be a genuine road towards contact, a way of getting to know somebody, a prelude to more profound exchanges, a simple and natural approach. But, let us admit it, it is also often used as a means of avoiding personal contact. It is like a prologue that goes on so long that the play never begins. It allows us to be friendly and interesting with people without touching on subjects that would compel us to enter into real dialogue.

(*The Meaning of Persons,* 143)

Each of us does his best to hide behind a shield. For one it is a mysterious silence which constitutes an impenetrable retreat. For another it is facile chit-chat, so that we never seem to get near him. Or else it is erudition, quotations, abstractions, theories, academic argument, technical jargon; or ready-made answers, trivialities,or sententious and patronizing advice.

One hides behind his timidity, so that we cannot find anything to say to him; another behind a fine self-assurance which renders him less vulnerable. At one moment we have recourse to our intelligence, to help us to juggle with words. Later on we pretend to be stupid so that we can reply as if we had not understood. It is possible to hide behind one's advanced years, or behind one's university degree, one's political office, or the necessity of nursing one's reputation. A woman can hide behind her startling beauty, or behind her husband's notoriety; just as, indeed, a husband can hide behind his wife.

A joke or a witty remark is always an easy way of breaking off an embarrassing dialogue. I am not here condemning wit, which is one of the graces of life. When I take up an illustrated journal the first thing I look at is the humorous cartoons. The vocation of the humorist seems to me to be eminently beneficent: he is able to get some valuable truth across much more directly and more delicately than the moralist.

(*The Meaning of Persons,* 143f.)

Work can be used as defensive shield. There are men who bring work home every evening so as to have an excuse for not entering into any serious conversation with their wives or children. Others barricade themselves behind the newspaper as soon as they get home, pretending to be deeply absorbed in it when their wives try to tell them of their troubles. Others put on the wireless. They have a concert to listen to or a match to follow just at the one moment when there might be a possibility of calmly discussing important and pressing decisions that have to be taken.

Often, without realizing it, a woman takes refuge from the dialogue in her domestic chores: she always has to do some ironing that cannot wait, or else she has to see that the children get on with their homework. By what amounts to a secret understanding many couples constantly avoid being alone together. They are always having visitors, or going to see a show. For their holidays they go off with a troop of friends.

(*The Meaning of Persons,* 144f.)

In every encounter, from the simplest conversation between two friends, a ladies' sewing party, a gentlemen's club, a committee meeting, to the assemblies of scientific associations and great international political conferences, arguments are put forward in apparently objective and rational debate; but in reality each speaker is taking up and defending positions dictated by his instincts, his affectivity and his archetypal tendencies. Beneath the intellectual discussion we are moved all the time by fears, jealousies, childish admirations, unconscious projections.

A spiritual or intellectual experience is always accompanied by an emotional experience. We feel joy at being united with others professing the same beliefs, people whom we love and who love us because we are engaged together in a common struggle. A person who has had this experience in a religious community or a political party, or through reading Karl Marx, St Thomas, Karl Barth or Rudolf Steiner, Freud, Bergson or Kierkegaard, will never tire of defending his master's system of thought, and will do it more passionately and uncompromisingly than the master himself. In such discussions how much real contact is there between the protagonists? How much real dialogue is there? It is rather a conflict of monologues, in which each is astonished that the logical arguments he is developing, which to him seem so compelling, do not at once convince the other.

Many a discussion would take quite a different course if we were to admit to each other the emotional and quite personal bases of our opinions: the bitterness against his father which turns a young man into an anarchist; the fear of losing his money which makes a rich man an adversary of communism; the jealousy which makes a committee-member oppose everything suggested by one of his colleagues; the desire for revenge which turns a young woman into a suffragette, because her father used to bully her mother, or which turns a man into an anti-feminist, because he is dominated by his wife.

(*The Meaning of Persons*, 55f.)

It is our own secrets that separate us the most from others: remorse for our wrongdoings, fears that haunt us, disgust with ourselves that we continually succumb to a certain recurring temptation, inner doubts so vividly in contrast with our air of self-confidence, our jealousy and our anger, and even the naïve daydreams of glory by which we console ourselves.

When people open up to us, we discover that their real remorse has to do with faults quite different from those for which others reproach them. Others aim criticism at their failings, but their own accusations are aimed at a deeper level of conscience, at the sin that is as a hidden source of their visible failings. At the level of their failings, we succeed only in humiliating them, for their great desire is to be free from these although they never succeed in freeing themselves; at the level of sin, we can lead them into the experience of liberation.

No one finds it easy to overcome the inner resistance that obstructs the way to a sincere and deep unveiling of himself.

(*Escape from Loneliness,* 45)

There is at every moment and in our relationships with every person, without our being aware of it, a small measure of our personal secrets that we reveal and a small measure that we keep. By that may be measured the maturity of a person, his personal freedom. Children who do not know how to keep a secret, chatterboxes, men or women who don't know where to stop, or cannot, are powerless to establish with others a proper person-to-person relationship. They cannot resist the vain pleasure of telling all sorts of secrets that they are proud to know, and because of their lack of inner freedom fall under the subjection of others. But close beings, incapable of expressing anything truly personal, are condemned to the prison of their mental solitude. Every being has need of self-expression. Why do men like to meet in a cafe, women in a tearoom, young people at a bar? They meet to tell each other their little secrets. There are some people who must be taught to speak out more and others who must be taught to keep quiet; and each is as difficult as the other.

(*Secrets,* 33)

Everyone has his own private thermostat. There are some people warmer than others; there are some more talkative, who endlessly tell innumerable secrets already known by everyone; there are others, more taciturn. There are some whose voices are only imperceptible murmurs; there are some so noisy they disturb everyone, and, in a restaurant, tell their secrets so loud that no one misses them. The Dutch don't have any curtains on their windows even in the evening. They like passers-by to see their sumptuous furniture, the inside of their home, their calm and model family life. The French surround their homes with high walls and close the blinds even during the day.

But there is something much more profound than these crude appearances. A Dutchman is no more ready to open his heart to someone than a Frenchman, a noisy person than a tactiturn. A truly intimate word from a man who is usually reserved bowls us over. And also it is for him the occasion of a much richer experience than a flood of secret revelations spread carelessly by someone else. Even silence has its different tonalities according to the moment. It can be a haughty refusal, but it can be a real gift of self.

(*Secrets*, 32)

In the life of each of us there are decisive hours that tell us more about the person than all the rest of our lives put together. Do I say hours? Minutes, seconds, rather; moments which are to determine the whole course of our lives thereafter.

Now, the cross-roads is this moment of true dialogue, of personal encounter with another person, which obliges us to take up a position with regard to him, to commit ourselves. Even to run away is to make some sort of decision, choosing a side-road in order to evade the dialogue. Most of the incessant fluctuations of our being and of our behaviour, actions and words are, as in the animals, merely reflex responses to an external stimulus, manifestations of the personage. At the moment of true dialogue, of inner personal communion, we cannot avoid taking up a position, and in this genuine responsible act the person is unveiled. That is why Sartre writes: 'I cannot know myself except through the intermediary of another person.'

(*The Meaning of Persons*, 129f.)

The highest sign of friendship is that of giving another the privilege of sharing your inner thought. It is a personal gift in which there is self-commitment.

(*The Meaning of Gifts*, 39f.)

Labels and appearances

To put a label on someone is inevitably to contribute to making him conform to the label, especially if the person is at the impressionable age of childhood. To treat him as a liar is to make him one, and it is the same with selfishness or pride. I no longer believe that there are bad characters – I do believe that there is sin, which is quite another matter. The first of these two concepts belongs to the realm of social formalism, the second to that of moral realism. We are all sinners – equally sinners: the decent, honourable, respectable folk equally with those they despise; and cruel, unjust, proud parents equally with the children they crush with this talk of bad characters.

(*The Strong and the Weak*, 57)

If one thoughtlessly calls a child a liar, one makes him a liar, in spite of all his aspirations towards honesty. He is still at the age when the frontier between myth and reality is imprecise. People tell him fairy-stories; and if he too invents stories, he tells them as if they had really happened, and finds himself called a liar.

Call a child stupid, and you make him stupid, incapable of showing what he has it in him to do. A very pretty girl may always have been told by her mother that she is plain, either in order to preserve her from becoming conceited, or else from a subconscious motive which operates more often than one might imagine, namely, fear that she might outshine her mother. The girl comes to have so little confidence in her looks that if a man stares at her she mistakes his admiration for scorn.

The power of suggestion exercised by the labels we are given is considerable. This is particularly the case in childhood, but the same is true throughout our lives.

(*The Meaning of Persons*, 50f.)

I should like with all my heart to be full of love for all my patients, for I know well that that is what they need most, and what Jesus Christ expects of me. I cannot escape the danger of trying to show it when I have not got it, of covering up criticism and irritation under a mask of amiability, the discordance of which an intuitive person is quick to note. Is this then the price that has to be paid in every noble vocation? *Noblesse oblige,* after all. The master must hide from his pupils the gaps in his knowledge. The barrister must show himself confident of success. The doctor would do grave harm to the morale of his patient where he to impart to him all his doubts about his diagnosis and prognosis. The university professor would not be considered a serious scholar unless he wrote a large number of books.

Sometimes we pretend to be in a hurry; at other times we act as if we had all the time in the world, in spite of our impatience. We do not dare to refuse to make a gift, because a certain person has asked us. We have our secret vanities which are much more naïve. I remember, shortly before receiving my doctorate, practising the new signature which I hoped soon to put into use, a complicated and artificial flourish which I soon abandoned.

(*The Meaning of Persons,* 38)

It would seem that nudists – at any rate some of them – sincerely pursue the paradisiac and utopian dream of a complete divesting of the formal personage in the hope of creating a more genuine human community. To reveal oneself in all simplicity, just as one is, without even hiding what elementary modesty prompts one to conceal, is meant to be the symbol of a renunciation of all hypocrisy. Often our patients tell us of dreams in which they have seen themselves naked, and this always represents an inner longing to cast away their mask. I speak of nudism only with caution, for it deserves a thorough study. But I have felt that in fact this 'idealist' dream of an innocent society is the mark of a psychological disturbance. This would explain the attraction exercised by nudism on people who suffer from unconscious repressions.

On this subject there is a passage in the Bible which is very much to the point. After the Fall, Adam and Eve provided themselves with a covering by sewing fig-leaves together to make aprons (Genesis 3.7). But God himself soon came and perfected their rudimentary art, making them clothing of skins (Genesis

3.21). For he knew that thenceforth, in our human condition, and until the redemption of the world should be accomplished, we might no more be completely naked persons. Instead of taking man's clothing away from him, God provides him with a finer garment. Later, St Paul, after exhorting us to put off the old man, invites us to put on the new man, born of the Spirit (Colossians 3.9–10). He speaks also of putting on the breastplate of righteousness, the helmet of salvation, and the girdle of truth (Ephesians 6.14–16).

So, with its characteristic realism, the biblical revelation turns us from the utopian dream of a life exempt from all appearance and all protection. For the efforts we were vainly making to isolate our person completely from our personage it substitutes a quite different idea: that of accepting the clothing which God himself gives us, of choosing our personage – the personage God wills us to have.

(*The Meaning of Persons*, 76f.)

Our personage moulds our person. The external role we play transforms us constantly, exerting its influence even on the deepest and most intimate recesses of the person. Of course, the habit does not make the monk – the proverb is an indication of the subtlety of the problem – putting on a dress will not turn us into a saint. But neither is it without good reason that a priest wears a cassock, a judge his robe, or the soldier his uniform. (Do you remember those August days of 1939, when the German radio played military marches from morning to night?) Napoleon knew what he was talking about when he wrote: 'One becomes the man of one's uniform.'

Propaganda comes to us from without, but it penetrates our deepest selves. The demeanour we adopt, every gesture we make, similarly play their part in fashioning us inwardly. It is actually possible to modify the character by a systematic reform of handwriting. Even our physical constitution is influenced by the personage we put on. Caricaturists know this well; I always remember a miser who looked as if he had been drawn by a particularly mordant caricaturist, with his nose and chin almost meeting, and his nails curved in a complete semicircle.

Thus our physical, psychical, and even our spiritual life bear the imprint of our personage.

(*The Meaning of Persons,* 80)

We are all equal in sin and in moral wretchedness. It is conventionalism which judges men by their social façade, whereas the gospel looks into the heart. This misleading classification is in fact propagated and cultivated by all those who wish to appear strong, in order to hide from themselves and others their secret weakness. We can take pride in retailing our victories and experiences, vaunt our social successes, proclaim the perfection of our philosophical, theological or sociological system, and claim to teach others the secret of happiness and virtue. We do it all in order to reassure ourselves. A system the solidity of which one takes pleasure in demonstrating is like a shelter in which one seeks security.

But we are well aware that along with our successes we have known defeat, and that no doctrine and no experience has been able to preserve us from it. And the further we advance in the Christian life the more we become aware of our sin. It is as if weights were continually being added to one of the pans of a balance; and each time this happens we need more of God's grace in the other pan in order to re-establish the equilibrium. But this equilibrium is always unstable, so that the very slightest weight is enough to upset it: discouragement and doubt are at our door. It is then that we are tempted to shut our eyes to our defeats, to go back to the old method of covering up by means of strong reactions – and the temptation is the greater the further we think we have advanced along the road of the spiritual life. But to do so would be at the same time to deprive ourselves of the grace which alone can redress the balance.

(*The Strong and the Weak,* 175f.)

Looking for freedom

We ought not to smile at the idea of identification. It is a normal phenomenon to which every one of us is subject, a powerful social force, and also a valuable outlet without which the instinct for adventure would do more serious damage, driving men and nations to undertake courses of action that might be a danger to themselves and to others. Everybody cannot be a cosmonaut – today at any rate; and when everybody can be it will no longer be an adventure. But everyone can participate in spirit in what is a thrilling episode in the great human adventure. This is legitimate and beneficial. National solidarity, of course, promotes identification, so that a Russian identifies himself more completely with a Soviet cosmonaut, and a citizen of the USA with an American. Hence the powerful attraction of the Olympic Games and the big international matches, when whole nations get as excited as if each individual were involved in a personal adventure. The ancients understood this quite well, and when he re-established the Olympic Games Baron de Coubertin provided modern nations with a means of uniting through their need for adventure, a need which might well drive them into conflict with one another. He ought to have been given the Nobel Prize for Peace.

(*The Adventure of Living*, 17)

If I speak neither the language of reason nor that of poetry, I speak by my glance, my smile, my silence, my gestures and the demeanour I adopt. Consider this, and you will see that there must always enter into these things some measure of convention, which varies with the country and the period. Even the lover in his transports uses such hackneyed expressions, such well-worn gestures, that the lady he loves, were she to remain cool and clear-headed, must think him a very third-rate actor. She would soon detect re-hashed Lamartine or Stendhal, or Hollywood, and would perhaps mistake his genuinely spontaneous utterances for conscious imitation.

Almost the only emotional manifestations which can escape the charge of artificiality are those which are really physiological, like tears. And even then – I have known many families where no one ever wept, even on occasions such as bereavement; and more than one man or woman has told me that they hesitated to come to see me for fear of weeping as they recounted their troubles. And yet it is with the sudden furtive tear or the almost imperceptible smile that one senses the presence of the person hidden behind the habitual personage. These people want to discover themselves, and they are at the same time afraid of uncovering themselves. I am told that in the Far East, where death is certainly not viewed in the same emotional light as with us, they make a great noise when a death has taken place, in order to drive evil spirits away; they use professional weepers, who have themselves no cause for sorrow, while those who are in sorrow do not weep. No civilization has paid such attention to the principle of saving face.

(*The Meaning of Persons*, 75f.)

There are two worlds, or ways of looking at the world, of entering into relationship with it, depending on the spirit in which we approach it. We may see in it nothing but things, mechanisms, from those of physics to those of biology and even of psychology. Art, philosophy, religion can also become things, collections of concepts, formulae, definitions. On the other hand, one can lay oneself open to the world of persons, awaken to the sense of the person. By becoming oneself a person one discovers other persons round about, and one seeks to establish a personal bond with them.

The person always eludes our grasp; it is never static. It refuses to be confined within concepts, formulae and definitions. It is not a thing to be encompassed, but a point of attraction, a guiding force, a direction, an attitude, which demands from us a corresponding attitude, which moves us to action and commits us. The world of things does not commit us. It is neutral, and leaves us neutral. We are cold, objective, impersonal observers, watching the operation of blind and inexorable mechanisms.

I am not claiming that we must shut our eyes to things, nor

that we should cut ourselves off from intellectual objectivity, from the fascinating study of the ordinances and mechanisms of things. But I ask that we should not limit ourselves to the study of things, for they are only one half of the world, the static, impassible, unfeeling half.

(*The Meaning of Persons,* 179f.)

I have no hesitation in saying – for I can observe it daily – that the majority of the psychological effects of religious faith are the effects of suggestion. This is a matter of their mechanism, which science investigates and calls the law of suggestion: that ideas tend to turn into facts. But do not let us confuse the mechanism with the cause. Whereas the law of suggestion explains the mechanism, it takes no account of the cause. Faith recognizes the intervention of God as the cause of the suggestion.

Like all natural laws, the law of suggestion is neutral in itself. It can be the source of the most terrible suffering, as well as of the most wonderful deliverances. It lies behind the chain reaction by virtue of which the ills as well as the blessings in a person's life tend always to increase. One misfortune suggests the fear of a new misfortune, and the fear precipitates the person into the very thing he fears. One stroke of good fortune suggests the expectation of another, and this attitude of expectancy brings it about. Christ was obviously alluding to this effect of the law of suggestion when he said: 'To him who has will more be given, and he will have abundance; but from him who has not, even what he has will be taken away' (Matthew 13.12).

(*The Person Reborn,* 144)

Everything that men and women think, all they believe, all they feel, depends on suggestions they have received, and on the processes of thought determined by those suggestions in their unconscious. They all believe they have personal convictions and thoughts. But their convictions and thoughts would not be the same if they had read different books, had met different people, had had different parents, had gone to different schools. They readily believe that general approbation is a guarantee of authenticity. It is not so long ago that certain moral concepts such as respect for the human person irrespective of race, for marriage and the family as opposed to free love, or the concept of law as being above all human will or power, were thought of as sacrosanct. They could be violated in practice, but in principle they could not be gainsaid. It has taken recent events to show us that this apparent unanimity, far from being based on a sort of moral instinct, was due to the force of social suggestion.

Even experience is not a conclusive proof of truth, because all that is required is an absolute belief in an idea, even if it is false, for the experience it inspires to be conclusive.

This is why people generally have an instinctive distrust of the power of suggestion, so that preaching and religious demonstrations always come up against a defensive and critical attitude among the hearers. They are afraid that their suggestibility is being played upon in order to make them believe things that are not true. They have so often been disappointed after taking something up in a surge of sincere enthusiasm.

Suggestion is simply a natural law: every idea, true or false, tends to propagate itself and become a fact. No doubt suggestion played its part in the spread of Christianity, in the success of many healing acts, in the courage of the martyrs, in many answers to prayer. But suggestion can quite as easily spread some other doctrine, unite immense multitudes in false beliefs, arousing equal dedication and heroism in them.

(*The Person Reborn,* 158)

The true question therefore is not, 'Is faith suggestion?' but, 'This mechanism of suggestion which, by God's will, holds sway over men – does it lead them into the truth or into error?' Or again, 'These ideas which spread and become actual experiences in accordance with the law of suggestion – do they come from God or the devil? And if science shows us that sometimes they come from the unconscious, do they come from what is healthy and godly in the unconscious, or from what is diabolical and pathological?'

All our behaviour has its source in ideas, and all our ideas have come to us from outside. They have been suggested to us by a good or a bad counsellor. They may derive from our selfishness, from our conscious or unconscious tendencies towards sensuality, pride, vanity, the exercise of power, hate or impurity. They may also come from God – from his call to love, in humility, honesty and self-sacrifice.

The whole drama of life arises from this perpetual concurrence of suggestions from God and those inspired by evil, the positive and the negative. This is why our hearts are always divided. Indeed, every positive idea awakens in us a negative echo. If I say: 'I believe in God', the echo replies: 'Are you really sure?' The two ideas go together and are propagated by the power of suggestion. The devil makes use of the resulting disorder for his own ends. He makes a person suffering from depression turn every encouraging remark we make into a negative suggestion. We say to him: 'You see, you are better.' He replies: 'You're surprised, aren't you? You must have given up all hope for me.'

But this very battle that takes place within us is a proof of the existence of God. If his voice did not sound within us, we should be altogether one-sided, and there would no longer be any battle!

(*The Person Reborn,* 160)

To be truly personal is to acquire liberty of conduct, to be, to some extent at least, able to govern oneself instead of being governed by automatisms. It is to be able to be generous or sparing as the changing circumstances require and in accordance with a conviction freely arrived at. It is to be able to be an idealist without losing sight of reality, to be a realist without betraying one's ideals. It is to be orderly without making such a fetish of order that the least disorder is a torture. In the nineteenth century appeal was made to the will. Modern psychology has shown how futile and even harmful is this dependence on our own efforts. All it leads to is the donning of a new artificial personage over the top of the first.

Furthermore, to depend on one's own will-power, one's good resolutions, especially against the impulsions of instinct and the determinism of powerful psychological complexes, is to ask for failure and for a perpetual conflict which will destroy rather than strengthen the forces of the person. It may be successful against a minor failing such as untidiness, but at the price of a new slavery: the slavery of one's own resolutions, which will leave no room for flexibility or for personal fancy. If any unforseen event should happen to upset the established order of things to which one clings, the result will be a state of anxiety.

(*The Meaning of Persons*, 222)

Many people have a quite negative conception of Christianity, as if it consisted in continual self-amputation, as if God wanted to hold us down, rather than that we should 'turn again and live'. Would such a God deserve the name of Father which Christ gave to him? When I labour to liberate a crushed life, I am not fighting against God, but with him. Like a gardener who removes from around a plant the weeds that choke it, using all the care that as one of God's creatures it deserves, I am helping to re-establish his purpose of life.

It is God who gave it life, and he surely wants it to flourish and bear fruit. Does not Christ often speak of bearing fruit? Bearing fruit means being oneself, asserting oneself, growing in accordance with God's purpose.

Christianity, therefore, has its positive, affirmative, creative aspect – ignored by many Christians. I do not deny that it imposes certain specific acts of renunciation. Jesus spoke of the husbandman who prunes his vine so that it may bear more fruit. The purpose of pruning is not to restrict life, but on the contrary to promote its fuller and richer flow.

Christian life, then, is liberty, the liberation of the person from the trammels imposed by external influences. It is the rising of the sap from within. It is life under God's leadership. It is a balance between prayer and action: between the dialogue in which his creative inspiration is sought, and the bold and confident affirmation of self, in which the inspiration received is put into practice.

(*The Meaning of Persons*, 226f.)

The God whom we know in Jesus Christ is known to others under widely varying names and attributes. They seek him in nature; they seek him in the truth pursued by science; they seek him in the social justice and international peace they are trying to create; when they are embarrassed by their own wrongdoing and try to hide it, they show they have some inkling of his sovereign demands; behind many of the upsets in their physical or psychic life they suspect that something in them, which they cannot name, but which does not come from either their bodies or their minds, is not what it ought to be. This something is what I call 'the spirit'.

Many people today are thinking about the crisis through which the world is passing. Although they are of the most varying beliefs, they are arriving at the same conclusions. They realize that modern civilization has lost its soul; that technical skill divorced from faith does not suffice to bring peace and happiness; that the spirit has been relegated to the narrow confines of the church and of private belief; that it has ceased to be a power in the real lives of men and women – in politics, economics, art and intellectual life. They believe that this is why the world is no longer able to find any solutions to the personal, family, national and international problems that beset it. If we try to make a particular orthodox belief the indispensable credential for anyone who wants to join in work for the spiritual reconstruction of the world, we shall turn away the majority of people of good will, whom we ought to be welcoming with open arms. Bring them our Christian convictions, but let us hold out the hand of friendship to them. We shall be able, without denying our faith, to find a basis for common action, for they, like us, believe in the spirit.

(*The Person Reborn*, 197f.)

Love

It was for love that God created the world. It was for love that God made man in his own image, thus making him a partner in love, a being to whom he speaks, whom he loves like a son, and who can answer him and love him like a father. It is for love that God respects man's liberty, thus taking upon himself the formidable risk of man's mistakes and disobediences, the price of which he himself accepts and pays in the sacrifice of the cross.

Love is also, in my view, the meaning of all human adventure. The instinct of adventure which God gave man in creating him in his own image is in fact, I believe, an instinct of love, a need to give himself, to dedicate himself, to pursue a worthwhile goal, accepting every sacrifice in order to attain it. This is the source of the joy of adventure, the joy of doing something, and of doing it for someone – for God who has called him to do it, if he is a believer, and in any case for mankind, to procure for mankind the benefits he is striving for. One is reminded of St Ignatius Loyola's beautiful words: 'We must make no important decision without opening our hearts to love.'

(*The Adventure of Living*, 92)

Women in general have the sense of the person much more than men have. This means that they have a special mission, which is to reintroduce love, to give back its humanity to a world which remains so glacial when men alone have built it.

(*What's in a Name?*, 86)

Really to love is to listen. It is not so long since in some circles it was the custom to forbid children to speak at the table. The adults' conversation flowed around them, and they were unable to take part in it. The same thing still happens with old people.

There are families in which both children and adults give noisy expression to their views, arguing and answering back over the heads of the old, who are given no opportunity to speak, because nobody bothers to think that they might have anything to say. They feel that they are looked upon as worn-out and of no further importance. Or else they are spoken to in a particular tone of voice, as used to be the case with the children, condescendingly, kindly, perhaps even affectionately, but in a way which indicates that no valid reply can be expected.

I have just read in a local paper, the Geneva *Messager social,* a well-written account of an interesting little scene in a teashop. A couple had kindly invited the wife's mother to have tea with them. The writer of the article, seated at the next table, was observing them. The husband and wife were in animated conversation with each other, but without ever addressing a single word to the old lady, except perhaps to say sweetly: 'Another cup of tea, mummy? Have another little piece of cake.' They were doing a kind act; they were bothering about their mother; they were taking her out with them. They seemed surprised that she remained passive, that she was not more effusive in her thanks. But doubtless a personal word would have meant more to her than fancy cakes.

(*Learning to Grow Old,* 62f.)

To love is to give one's time. We never give the impression that we care when we are in a hurry. Too many social and pastoral counsellors are people in a hurry. Hence, people admire their devotion and doubt their love. I am ever struck by the tranquillity in which Christ walked along, always having time to speak with a poor woman beside a well, or replying to the stupid questions of his disciples the very eve of his passion. To exercise a spiritual ministry means to take time. If we want to save our time for more important matters than a soul, we are but tradesmen. A colleague once said to me, 'I don't understand how you find patience to listen to these interminable stories without any interest which people force upon us.' If he only knew how it becomes interesting, once we become interested in people!

(*Escape from Loneliness,* 116)

Love needs to be demonstrated, to find expression in gifts, both personal and ritual gifts. Many people look down upon our common traditions, politeness, gallantry, things which they call hollow and formalistic make-believe. But let no one fool you: there is deep meaning in such customs. They are intended to please, and in pleasing others to afford a real pleasure in living to the person who is acting.

(*The Meaning of Gifts,* 50)

Love is not just some great abstract idea or feeling. There are some people with such a lofty conception of love that they never succeed in expressing it in the simple kindnesses of ordinary life. They dream of heroic devotion and self-sacrifice. But, waiting for the opportunity that never comes, they make themselves very unlikeable to those near them and never sense their neighbours' need for affection.

To love is to will the good for another. Love may mean writing with enough care so that our correspondent can read without spending time deciphering; that is, it may mean taking the time to save his time. To love is to pay one's bills; it is to keep things in order so that the wife's work will be made easier. It means arriving somewhere on time; it means giving your full attention to the one who is talking to you. To miss what he says means that we are more interested in what we are telling ourselves inwardly than in what he is telling us. To love is to try to speak in his language, even if we have mastered it but poorly, rather than to force him to speak ours.

(*Escape from Loneliness,* 115)

Love always means going to others, not demanding that they come to us. Nothing is more tragic and cruel than the spiritual tyranny we meet so often. He who has had a rich experience wants to impose it upon others, no holds barred, in order to save them. However, he does not realize the infinite variety of ways by one of which each person needs to find freely what he is seeking. He is unaware of the spirit of judgment and pride that permeates his effort at religious instruction and that soon impedes his work.

(*Escape from Loneliness,* 109)

It is always those who have the deepest hurt to forgive who forgive the most completely. Hatred and love are two emotions very, very close to one another. If we symbolize hatred with a negative quantity, –n, forgiveness is not just the cancellation of the wrong which would create an emotional neutrality, o; rather, it is a change from minus to plus, in quantity. Forgiveness is the replacement of hatred by love, +n. He who cannot hate intensely cannot love deeply. Thus the same intuitive insight which tracked down the wrong in all its wrongness, can also come to see the tragic state of the guilty conscience.

(*Escape from Loneliness*, 155)

There can be no question of denying the animal in us, of disowning this highly developed machine which reacts perfectly adequately to every stimulus. It is the mainstay of our existence. But if that is all there is in me, I am not a man. Love, for example, in so far as it can be studied scientifically, is merely a natural function. Whether it be the sex instinct, the maternal instinct, or simple emotional states, or the need to love and be loved, which the animal feels as much as we do, these are still nothing more than automatic reactions to external stimuli.

But when love suddenly springs up when we least expect it – love for a hostile individual substituted for the natural aggressive riposte, prompting forgiveness, displacing self-interest – then we are in the presence of a creative act that is really free and undetermined. It is a bursting forth of life, a positive choosing of a new direction, breaking the chain of natural reactions.

This is action properly so called, truly spontaneous and creative, and as such it remains isolated, unique and unforeseeable – and so impossible to study scientifically. It is a manifestation of the person thrusting aside the personage. But it will become in its turn the source of a new set of automatic reactions to a multitude of situations, reactions which will be accessible to the objective examination of psychology. They will be the evidence of the new force that is at work, just as we may be certain that there is a locomotive drawing the line of waggons we can see moving on the horizon, even though it may be hidden from view.

(*The Meaning of Persons*, 98)

Love has its natural and its supernatural aspects. But where is the dividing line? To oppose spiritual love to natural love is to render love unincarnate; it is to make the false antithesis between the spirit and the flesh which has done so much harm among religious people, to fail to recognize what there is of the divine in the 'libido'. But how many people are there who have deluded themselves by taking for a spiritual communion what is no more than an amorous transport, by imagining themselves to be possessed by a spiritual love when in fact they are actuated only by a more or less conscious natural lust?

(*The Strong and the Weak*, 214)

One can embrace the object of one's love so strongly that one crushes him to death. Hate can kill, we all know. Policemen were invented to curb its murderous effects. But love also can kill, and there are no policemen who can deal with that.

(*What's in a Name?*, 48)

From the psychological standpoint, it may be observed that all human conflicts are in the last analysis lovers' quarrels. People fight as fiercely as they do because both sides are convinced that they are fighting for a cause worthy of their love – for country, justice, or truth. This is true even of their conflicts with God, when they shake their fists at heaven. It is because they are disappointed in their need to love and be loved that they hurl themselves into the worst kind of adventures – into war and revolution. That is why there is always something noble in any revolt: a thrust towards an ideal, an outburst of adventurous energy, in which men commit their highest capacity for love.

(*The Adventure of Living*, 93)

Gifts

Men have an avid thirst for gifts. It is very evident in their great rush to clearance sales and bargain days, and equally so in their pleasure in purchasing some object which they really do not need, but which they've purchased simply because it cost 'practically nothing'. Again we see the thirst for gifts in their desire for 'favours', free tickets, special privileges thanks to a friend, and every other kind of gatecrashing. Is it not interesting to look upon the whole of economic life from this point of view? Not just as an instinctual need to procure for oneself the means of subsistence, but equally as a universal, spiritual need for exchanging with others: in other words, to see it as the need for interpersonal contact!

(*The Meaning of Gifts*, 33)

In some respects the great quest for gifts is a means by which we deceive ourselves, and by our little gifts we numb our longing for the greater ones which escape us. And yet, despite this, the concept of a greater happiness to come, mysterious and yet real and complete, stands out beyond all this race after incomplete and partial gifts and indeed gives it meaning. If each gift is a symbol of love, no matter how small the gift, then surely there must be a love, total and supreme, one that doesn't fail. This is what men intuitively await, and what they are seeking in the smallest gifts received each day. It is as if successive little payments assure us of the final payment-in-full. Sooner or later we realize that all human gifts are relative, limited and uncertain, even the most beautiful and costly of them. Everything that we receive we can also lose. Men can always deny the love which they have been offering, and as we have seen, their gifts are never completely free of other motives: pride, self-interest, or the desire to dominate. This is why the hunger is not assuaged. There must always be new gifts to complete and confirm those already received. This persisting need is itself a clear indication that its goal is ever towards a final ending after which we all confusedly aspire. We are looking for an absolutely unchanging love, one that nothing can ever change. The universal quest for gifts is nothing other than a seeking after God, by whatever name we may call him. For only the One who has made all things and who owns all things can give them without asking anything in return except our gratitude.

(*The Meaning of Gifts,* 58f.)

One can dominate others through gifts. Herein lies another chapter of their multiple meanings. When we present an unexpected gift, we have already gained a feeling of power which is delicious to our taste as we hear the exclamations, 'Oh! You shouldn't have done it! Is it really for me?' A beautiful gift enhances the one who gives. It can enhance also the recipient, but the temptation to dominate is strong. The gift which is too wonderful does not honour the one who receives; it humiliates him. One which goes beyond ordinary social conventions gives us quickly the feeling of being trapped, of becoming obligated to the giver, especially if we have no means of doing the same for him. In short, it alienates us. Generally, the people who enjoy most distributing gifts generously about are the very people who shy away most from accepting gifts. They are adamant on paying precisely their share of a shared trip, adding often, 'Good accounts make for good friends.'

(*The Meaning of Gifts,* 28)

The more unexpected and personal the gift, the more it touches the heart, but this emotion is not always easily expressed. The more necessary and traditional the saying of a thank-you, the more difficult it is, even when it is sincere. Charity loses its impetus when it is organized and conventional. Just as you give with joy to a cause, a church or a person, if there is a living relationship between you and that cause or person, in the same way your giving is debased to a burden when it becomes a regular and obligatory deduction from your bank account.

(*The Meaning of Gifts,* 43)

Advice

Advice is the only form of social activity of which many are capable of conceiving. Those whom life has wounded have met givers of advice on every hand. Often the advice is good, but if they follow it, they remain children. If they do not follow the advice given, they are isolated. Often they are surprised that I do not give them any advice. They would prefer at times to be led rather than to assume personal responsibility for themselves. Thus I patiently apply myself to giving back self-confidence to the client who has completely lost it. It is very important that he dare to affirm his own personal conviction.

(*Escape from Loneliness*, 166)

Advice may put people back together again, but it cannot change them. 'Advice which can touch only upon the manner of action,' said Ariston of old, 'can never transform the soul and set it free from its false opinions.' Advice touches the surface of personality, not the centre. It calls for an effort of the will, whereas the true cure of souls aims at the renewal of the inner affections.

(*Escape from Loneliness*, 166f.)

The more we study the human mind and learn to know its secret motivations, the more sincerely, even, we try to recognize the real and often murky currents in our own hearts, the more do we develop in ourselves a psychological and moral clairvoyance. We discover in fact that sins are often hidden behind what we thought were good qualities, and that genuine treasures of the mind underlie what we have looked upon as failings. This perspicacity can, however, be used for both good and evil, depending on the spirit that animates us. It is for good if we use it in order to unmask ourselves and to understand others. It is for evil if we use it in order to justify ourselves, and criticize others. And so the study of psychology may wonderfully fertilize the ministry of soul-healing in a person who is inspired by a true vocation of love. It can also turn the practitioner into a misanthrope and a pitiless critic, seeing only evil everywhere, even in those who are most sincere and well-intentioned.

(*The Person Reborn,* 59)

Every light casts a shadow; in everything we do for the good of a person's soul we run in some degree the risk of taking God's place there.

(*A Doctor's Casebook,* 112)

Perhaps I should be doing violence to the truth if I said that God speaks to me through every book I read. Nevertheless, there is something here of that attitude of which I was speaking just now when I said that the believer is always 'listening-in' to God. Similarly, my patients very often say to me: 'I admire the patience with which you listen to everything I tell you.' It is not patience at all, but interest. Everything is of absorbing interest to the person who is always looking for the meaning of things. There is so much to learn from the least important case if one is animated by this spirit of curiosity. There are no ordinary cases. All the greatest problems of human destiny are fundamentally present in the life of every person and in every situation we meet.

(*A Doctor's Casebook,* 40)

A religious experience is like a revolution. A prince has taken over a country by means of a *coup d'état.* Among the crowd that acclaims him, the followers of the fallen monarch, who is now powerless, are for the moment the most zealous partisans of the new ruler. But their change of heart is not sincere, and they are the enemy who will secretly scheme the gradual undermining of the new regime. If the reigning prince wins some triumph, they bow down and pretend to submit, only to raise their heads once again at the first opportunity to undermine his power.

This is what happens in the case of the submerged elements in our mental make-up. They hide themselves away when we are winning spiritual victories. They camouflage themselves and share in the inner unanimity we feel. But they have certainly not capitulated, and they succeed in sabotaging those victories if we do not unmask them. The process of unmasking them is a slow one, and is a matter of medical technique.

But the state police is wasting its time pursuing the conspirators if the monarch does not use the security thus won to accomplish his task nobly.

(*The Person Reborn,* 6f.)

We continually mistake instruction for thinking. As soon as a man begins to commune with himself, even though he may have had little formal education, he discovers that he can make his brain work just as much as the intellectual. He realizes that he can muster his imagination and his creative thinking to the service of his community. He is no longer limited to criticisms. We must admit it: mental laziness is one of the most widespread defects of our people.

(*Escape from Loneliness,* 173)

As long as a man is accused by the law, by society, by *other people,* he defends himself; it is a universal reflex. This defensive attitude prevents him from 'coming to himself' and undergoing a moral experience. In the belief that it is leading him towards such an experience, society is in fact leading him away from it. But as soon as *other people,* instead of casting stones at him, recognize that in the perspective of the heart they are as guilty as he, he accuses *himself,* he repents and undergoes that moral experience which the Gospel calls salvation.

So where others are concerned: total absence of responsibility. Where we ourselves are concerned: total responsibility.

I belive that in thus formulating my views I am being true to the spirit of the gospel. When Jesus' disciples asked him if a blind man was born blind because of his own sin or that of his parents, Jesus replied categorically: 'No' (John 9.2–3). Similarly, he asked his disciples, on the subject of an accident: 'Those eighteen upon whom the tower in Siloam fell and killed them, do you think that they were worse offenders than all the others who dwelt in Jerusalem? I tell you, No; but unless you repent you will all likewise perish' (Luke 13.4–5). So, when it was matter of the sins of *others*, he denied their responsibility; but where *their own* sin was concerned, he affirmed it.

(*The Person Reborn*, 118)

Good and bad

Taking the Gospel seriously means taking its absolute demands seriously. It means the realization that the demands of Christianity are total. It calls us to sanctity; that is, to true morality and not to the moralism of conventional respectability. Sanctity does not involve believing oneself to be perfect – quite the reverse. On the plane of true morality, it involves the recognition of everything in our secret intentions and actions that is contrary to Christ's demand for honesty, purity, selflessness, and love. It means refusing to compromise with those secret desires, and renouncing them.

We do not, as so many Christians as well as non-Christians think, seek this honest self-knowledge in order to make ourselves more virtuous – that is not at all what results. We do so in order to achieve closer fellowship with the Spirit, in an atmosphere of greater honesty. We do so in order to receive this blessing from God, which is more precious than all else because it procures in our personal lives victories which our unaided efforts have been powerless to achieve, besides increased effectiveness in our social activities. Thus our inward and our outward adventures are indissolubly bound up together.

What we can do for others and for the world at large must always begin in ourselves. Christian revolution always goes deeper than any ideological revolution because its roots are in a change of heart.

(*The Person Reborn*, 203)

One might say that from time to time in history the absolute standard is lost and then rediscovered. Under the guidance of the Spirit, believers become aware of it once again, and feel how hollow their petty conventional morality is in the face of God's demand for total self-giving and his concern with what is in men's hearts. Then all at once they are liberated from formal moralism, and are led to a personal discipline that is infinitely more severe. Then the flame of the Spirit gradually fades and the living, burning, free morality which they have forged becomes crystallized once more in hollow traditions and a narrow formalism that crushes the spirit, and to which people submit without any real, lively conviction in their hearts. The church slips back into scholasticism, and loses much of its influence upon society. What is needed then is the rediscovery of the absolute standard of the morality taught by the Christian gospel.

Without wishing to over-systematize, since these problems are applicable to all periods of time, I believe that we are at a period in which the religious world stands in urgent need of this rediscovery. To our contemporaries, churchmen seem to be self-satisfied, content to observe a few normal principles, to engage in theological debates, and to practise traditional forms of piety, none of which has any influence on their real lives. They become lost in minor scruples and fail to observe their complete failure in large and all-important areas of Christian morality. They appear to put their trust in a doctrine of gradual improvement, and no longer look for the revolutionary explosion of the Gospel, which bursts wide open the compromises of society.

(*The Person Reborn*, 60f.)

We can say that many of the events in a person's life are good or bad only in accordance with the spirit in which they are accepted or undergone.

On the formal level we classify events as being good or bad according to whether they are favourable to us or not. This is, of course, true. But on a deeper level, it is our underlying attitude to them that matters. We suffer an injustice; if we are made rebellious by it, it arouses evil in our hearts; if we can bear it unselfishly, it becomes, on the contrary, the occasion of a rich inner experience. We win a success: if it provokes us to pride, it is fatal for us; if it makes us work even harder, it is good. Seen from this angle, objectively, good events are sometimes revealed as harmful, while others, thought to be bad, turn out to have good results. Everything can be useful, and everything can be harmful, according to the spirit in which a person reacts. The spirit of formal moralism leads to the accentuation of external events, the spirit of true morality leads to the realization of personal responsibility. Both are right, because everything in this world has a twofold cause, external and internal.

(*The Person Reborn*, 53)

The most wonderful thing in this world is not the good that we accomplish, but the fact that good can come even out of the evil that we do. I have been struck, for example, by the numbers of people who have been brought back to God under the influence of a person to whom they had some improper attachment. I once read the diary of a lady of good family, which was a poignant record of such a case. Another lady, long after she had acknowledged her fault and had been forgiven for it, and having achieved a genuine sublimation of the passion that had been awakened in her, found herself being told one day: 'You must have been very much in love with someone once, to be able to be so loving toward everybody without making any distinction.' Love is so close to mysticism that even when it is illicit it can uplift the soul and lead to faith. Many people are disturbed by this. It disturbs them that adultery can bring true liberation to some people, because their own marital fidelity has been more a matter of convention and fear of 'what people might say', than of love of God's commandments. The world is too ready to throw stones at such people, and to cast doubts on the genuineness of the faith thus rediscovered. But is it not of more value than the seeming probity of the respectable man who, so often, 'commits adultery in his heart' (Matthew 5.28)? Moreover this new-found faith, provided that the Holy Spirit nurtures it, will not be long in bearing fruit in the form of a crisis of conscience, in which the sin that has been its cradle will be overcome.

(*The Person Reborn*, 81)

Taboos, much criticized by the psychologists, served a useful purpose in safeguarding people from moral anarchy. It is one of the tragedies of our time that on the one hand those who uphold the principles of morality do so on thoroughly conventionalist grounds, the dangers of which we have seen; whereas on the other hand, in the name of sincerity, or of a mission to remake the world, others set at nought the intangible laws of morality. It cannot be denied that the great increase in the number of cases of nervous disease is a consequence of the distress arising from being caught between these two extremes.

(*The Person Reborn*, 82)

It is in the form of alternatives that our problems first appear to us. We cannot formulate problems in any other than intellectual language. Now the property of intellectual language is its dilemma – either this or that – either I fight or I surrender. The one seems to exclude the other. The intellect reasons about a situation as if it were fixed and unchangeable. But what escapes intelligence is life itself, movement, change in people which changes the given elements of the problem and which tears us from the prison-grasp of the syllogism. Then, resistance and surrender no longer are opposites; one can both fight and compromise, so to speak, at the same time. Rather, one no longer needs either to give in or to fight on in the way he imagined before.

(*To Resist or to Surrender*, 56f.)

Instead of asking, 'Shall I resist or shall I give in?' we should sometimes ask ourselves a much more penetrating question. 'If I give in, is it willingly, or against my desires? If I hold out, is it out of conviction, or not?' Even so, it is often most difficult for us to answer these questions with certainty. How many people there are, many of the most capable, who remain perplexed and who, once their decision is made, cannot tell if it was freely made or if they were moved by unconscious motives.

(*To Resist or to Surrender*, 16)

On the way

The really important thing in life is not the avoidance of mistakes, but the obedience of faith. By obedience, the man is led step by step to correct his errors, whereas nothing will ever happen to him if he doesn't get going.

(*Escape from Loneliness*, 170)

There are people who go on indefinitely preparing for life instead of living it. They never feel that they are sufficiently well prepared, or strong enough. They go on studying for one thing after another, adding diploma to diploma, taking endless precautions. They fondly imagine that in this way they are improving their chances of success, but in reality all their effort is merely a compensation for lack of self-confidence. The only result of so much preparation is that their self-doubt increases and their chance of success is less than ever. We often see the same thing in our patients' dreams. It is time to leave on a journey, and the dreamer wastes time looking for some superfluous item; he packs so much into his suitcases that they will not close; he runs all the way to the station, but his luggage is so heavy and cumbersome that he is late, he gets stuck with his luggage as he tries to pass through the barrier, and the train moves out before his eyes.

(*The Adventure of Living,* 117)

One must adapt one's life to one's temperament. Those who are not gifted with boundless energy often over-work because they are afraid of being thought lazy or of being accused of molly-coddling themselves.

(*The Strong and the Weak*, 101)

Life is not a state, it is a movement. Nowhere in nature does it present the character of a fixed and stable maximum, but rather of an undulation, successive waves of life. Sincerity, as we have seen, is not a perfected state, but a movement experienced just at the point at which one perceives that one lacks it. Love is not a state, it is a movement. Personal contact is not a state, but a fleeting movement that must be ceaselessly rediscovered. Marriage is not a state, but a movement – a boundless adventure.

Nor is spiritual life a state. Faith is a movement towards God, a turning back towards God which one feels at the very moment when one confesses that one has turned away. That is why Jesus Christ compared the spirit to the wind, of which one does not know 'whence it cometh, and whither it goeth', to a force that passes, which cannot be laid hold of by the hands, and yet which quenches our thirst for the Absolute.

The person too is something that is uncompleted and evades our grasp. It imparts movement to our being, always refashioning our body and soul. The flowering of the person is not a state at which we arrive, it is the movement that results from perpetual incompleteness. If that flowering were the final stage of development, it would be also the halting of life. The rose that is in full bloom is already beginning to fade. Nor is the blossoming of the person, as so many people think, an accumulation of knowledge and experience, as it were stones placed one upon another to form a monument. The only result of that would be a grandiose personage, not a person.

The person belongs to the realm of quality, not quantity. It is suddenly manifested in a powerful inner movement which partakes of the nature of the Absolute. However many things we accumulated, that would bring us no nearer to it. The person resides in being, not in having. It is beyond all measure; it eludes every test; it is outside all definitions. The claim to self-knowledge is the surest road to a misunderstanding of self.

(*The Meaning of Persons*, 230f.)

Our personality is not static; it is the result of innate tendencies and of physical factors which we owe to our heredity. But it is also the result of the whole of our experience, of the teaching we have received, of the influences under which we have come, of the people we have met, of the books we have read and the films we have seen. And with each new day, even on a desert island, our personality will go on changing.

The intangible thing, it seems to me, is not the personality but the person; that which is immutable in us; that which is or is not; that which is specifically human, distinguishing the man from the animal. We are no more than animals if our freedom of choice and our sense of responsibility are taken from us; if we are deprived of our right to choose the influences which will modify our personality, and, in the last analysis, our right freely to obey or disobey God. We are persons when these possibilities and this right are safeguarded. For this reason, to speak of the person and of respect for the person, is to speak, not of that man which is physical, psychological or intellectual, but of what is spiritual in him, his moral conscience, his sense of responsibility, his freedom of choice.

(*A Doctor's Casebook*, 49f.)

The price that has to be paid for finding truly personal life is a very high one. It is a price in terms of the acceptance of responsibility. And the awareness of responsibility inevitably leads either to despair or to confession and grace. More is needed than the good intentions of the humanist. What is required is a new outlook, a personal revolution, a miracle.

The man who keeps secret his most painful memories, his bitterest remorse and his most private convictions, must needs show also, in his whole demeanour and in all his relationships with other people, a certain reserve which they all intuitively feel. This reserve is contagious, and sets up an obstacle to the development of personal relationships. On the other hand, the liberation experienced by the man who has confessed his sins is also contagious, even if he says nothing about the burden that has been lifted from his shoulders. All who come into contact with him find themselves becoming more personal. In order to build a personal world we need persons, men reborn into a life of freedom and responsibility. This second birth is not the fruit of our own resolve, any more than our first birth was. It comes by grace, through the encounter with God, through dialogue with him.

(*The Meaning of Persons*, 158)

It is utopian to think that we can live free of all complexes. We are always finding old reactions reappearing in us when we thought we had been freed from them. Living in grace is not the same as living in cotton-wool. He who has tasted grace can no longer be content with compromises, escapism or psychological compensations. He is constrained to confront all life's problems courageously, and faithfully to do battle with them.

Often, what we believe to be the most characteristically personal thing about us is in reality impersonal, since it is automatic. We are simply the slaves of certain impulses that result from psychological mechanisms entrenched in us by habit. One is a slave to his avarice, another to his prodigality. Both feel uneasy; both have a vague sense of being determined by their complexes, and thus of not being free, of betraying their persons instead of being personal. That this is so is shown by their constant need to reassure and justify themselves. The miser justifies his avarice by criticizing the spendthrift, and the spendthrift justifies his prodigality by criticizing the miser. All systematic criticism of a person or a group of persons is an indication either of jealousy or of some other personal complex.

(*The Meaning of Persons*, 221f.)

There are people who constantly defend themselves against those they most admire, for fear of their own personality being swamped. And this very attitude of perpetually being on the defensive is what prevents the free development of their personality. One can make a clean break with everything without being any more oneself as a result.

(*The Strong and the Weak*, 197)

The fact that a shy person has won a victory over his shyness does not mean that he is saved for all eternity. These victories in the order of earthly things are, as St Paul says, but an earnest of the great deliverance which we shall know only in heaven. Though the drunkard gives up drinking, he remains for all that a sinner. But the freeing of a man from a particular sin is a demonstration of the incomparable power of the Spirit.

(*The Strong and the Weak*, 208)

While a sacrifice can bear much fruit when it is a free response to the inner call of the spirit, it can also be sterile and destructive when it is merely a psychological reaction.

(*The Strong and the Weak*, 148)

Science and faith

The inorganic world may be compared to a train which is compelled by the rigid rails on which it runs to follow exactly a pre-established course. The world of living things, on the other hand, is like a motor-car which enjoys a certain margin of deviation from side to side on the road. Its course is kept practically straight by means of continual corrections to right or left applied through the steering wheel. Without this regulation the car would finish up in the ditch. But the regulation is a supple one, needing an intelligent driver, not an inflexible rail.

Claude Bernard himself wrote: 'The organism is regarded as a machine, and that is right; but it is considered as a fixed, immovable, automatic machine, confined within precise mathematical limits, and that is quite wrong. The organism is an organic machine, endowed, that is to say, with a flexible, elastic mechanism.' So, compared with the inorganic world, the living being enjoys a certain margin of deviation from the line of its course, and it is just this which makes it a living being. Its life is maintained by these perpetual fluctuations regulated by organic sensitivity.

(*The Meaning of Persons*, 92f.)

It is in fact through the development of his mind that man has raised himself above the animals. His inquisitiveness, his eternal dissatisfaction, his yearning for the absolute, have given rise to philosophy, science and theology. His emotional yearnings have given rise to society, and from them spring his spiritual experiences. But let this differentiation of his intelligence and his feelings get out of proportion, and man becomes unsuited for life, unsociable, incapable of loving, of being happy, of doing any useful intellectual work. What he needs is a new birth that will give him the soul of a child once more.

(*The Person Reborn*, 88)

It seems to me that man can always be looked at from two points of view: from the technical and scientific on the one hand, and from the spiritual and moral on the other. I think that each of these two points of view gives a true but incomplete picture of man. As in a pair of stereoscopic photographs, both pictures are true, but neither of them separately gives the lifelike view of the subject that is obtained by looking at them together in the stereoscope. Nevertheless, the fusion of the two images into a lifelike picture demands a difficult effort of visual adjustment. Similarly, it would seem that our minds are too circumscribed to see man at the same time in his mechanistic as well as his spiritual aspect, and to fuse these two partial views into a single living synthesis.

(*The Person Reborn*, 22)

I once saw in an Italian railway station a poster advertising some product or other under the name 'Cervino'. The picture on the poster represented the Matterhorn, which as a French-speaking Swiss, I had known as Mont Cervin. The picture had attracted my attention, however, because there was something odd about it. I soon realized what it was: it was the Matterhorn seen from the Italian side, with its peak pointing to the right. As a Swiss I was always used to seeing it with the point toward the left. I remember thinking that here was a sort of parable of the irreconcilable double aspect that I am describing here; two images, both true, but incapable of being seen both at the same time. You cannot view the Matterhorn from the Italian side and from the Swiss side at the same time. Nevertheless it is still the same mountain.

But just as it is possible with the stereoscope, using an optical device and visual effort, to fuse the two images into a more lifelike one, so we can use intuition in an attempt to form a synthesized concept of man, in which his two aspects are fused into one.

(*The Person Reborn*, 23)

Science studies each physical phenomenon, and the laws of immediate cause and effect relating to it, in isolation, each on its own level. But consideration of the whole process, of the phenomenon of phenomena itself, is beyond the scope of science. At that level intuition alone tells us that there must be a cause that transcends the whole, since it obeys an ordered plan. Science gives answers to the immediate questions. Why does the earth revolve around the sun? Because the sun exerts an attraction upon it. But to the overriding question of why there is a universal law of gravitation, science has no answer. Faith alone replies that it is because Someone has given the universe all its laws in order to fulfil his purpose thereby.

The universal process is, one might say, like a chain attached at one end to the ship and at the other to the quayside. If you ask why a particular link is where it is, analytical science will study its relationship with the links to right and left of it. That this immediate relationship determines its position is an objective mathematical fact. But if, on a diffferent scale, the chain is viewed as a whole, that link is seen to be an integral part of a series of links having a direction and a purpose which are in accord with the will of the sailor who placed the chain there in order to attach the ship to the quay. This too is a fact, a mediate fact, imparting a transcendent purpose to the immediate relationships of the individual links.

(*The Person Reborn*, 26f.)

Every new discovery of science brings to light an original invention by God, an ingenious solution found by him to each of the technical problems raised by the functioning of the world and of all its component parts, of all the heavenly bodies, of all the physical and chemical reactions of matter, and of every living organism. It is in this connection, perhaps, that we can sense most keenly the atmosphere of adventure which surrounds his creative enterprise. What ingenuity! He does not present us with only one solution to a technical difficulty but with ten, twenty or thirty. He invents feathers so that birds may fly, but he makes bats fly without feathers, and insects with a countless variety of membranes. And look at all the other means of locomotion he has invented: the fish that swims, the quadruped that gallops, the flea that jumps, the snake that crawls, and man walking upright on his two feet. He can transform fingernails into claws or into hooves. Think of the various means by which the dissemination of seeds is assured, of the means by which weak plants avail themselves of external aids in order to hold themselves up. Consider all the examples of symbiosis, the nitrogen cycle which makes animals tributaries of plants, the carbon atom which permits the numberless combinations of organic chemistry, the successive essays in visual organs, the various methods of reproduction in living things and the wonderful invention of sex, with all the differentations it makes possible.

(*The Adventure of Living*, 89)

The notion that science and faith conflict does not seem to me to be biblical. The Bible tells us of the institution of science as a gift from God. When God created man he commmanded him to give names to 'every beast of the field, and every fowl of the air' (Genesis 2.19). The giving of names is the basic principle of science. It is the function of natural science to give a clearly-defined name to each living species, as also to each chemical element and each physical force.

(*A Doctor's Casebook*, 26)

The foundation of science may also be seen in the unique power given by God to man and woman when he said to them: 'Replenish the earth, and subdue it; and have dominion over the fish of the sea, and over the fowl of the air, and over every living thing that moveth upon the earth' (Genesis 1.28). There is a passage in the Epistle of St James that should be compared with this text (James 3.7–8). He speaks of the tongue, of its misdeeds, and of man's inability to tame his own tongue, although he has tamed every kind of animal. The whole drama of science is present in this paradox: man controls nature, but does not control himself. The Bible condemns neither science nor man's power: it presents them as gifts of God which man must manage in submission to his Creator. The catastrophes brought about by science are not, in fact, the work of science, but that of the untamed heart of man using his power against God.

(*A Doctor's Casebook*, 26f.)

Science studies the laws of nature. It establishes, for instance, that the orbits of the heavenly bodies, the way things fall, and the movement of the tides all obey the same law of universal gravitation. But it does not know why there is a law of gravitation. It studies the mechanics of the evolution of species, but it does not know why there is an evolution by which all things move in a given direction. Similarly it studies the law of suggestion, but it does not know why there is a law of suggestion.

Faith believes that there are laws in nature because they have been laid down by someone whom it calls God, and that it is of him and not of his creatures that we must ask the reason why.

There is a difference between the laws of the inanimate world, like that of gravitation, and the laws of the mind, like that of suggestion. In the inanimate world the will of God is fulfilled of necessity, so that everything is good, since it obeys the laws he has established.

In the world of the mind, as is shown by the existence of evil, arising from the fact that God has left man free to obey him or disobey him, one and the same mechanism, set in motion by the God-given law of suggestion, can serve either obedience or disobedience. It can help to spread either truth or error, good or evil.

(*The Person Reborn*, 158f.)

The farmer sows his wheat in the grey days of autumn.

He knows in the springtime his field will be green with thousands of little shoots, and that in summer it will turn to the gold of harvest.

He knows this because from time immemorial this phenomenon has been observed. Science can analyse this; it can study every phase of germination, growth and fructification. It creates techniques which will increase the yield.

Faith consists in the recognition that it is God who makes the grain grow, and in loving and glorifying him in thanksgiving.

Impiety consists in deriding God while at the same time counting upon having bread next year.

Our gluttony has made us eat too much, and we have a headache. We know that the pain will disappear if we take a pain-killing tablet. Science can study the pharmacodynamic effect of the remedy, improve it, and increase its efficacy.

Faith consists in seeing this effect, which is still essentially a mystery to us, as a blessing from God – in our thanking him for it and repenting of our gluttony.

Impiety consists in thinking that we can give free rein to gluttony, thanks to the miracles of science, which will preserve us from its uncomfortable consequences.

A spiritual experience frees us from some functional trouble which has been weighing on our lives, perhaps excessive shyness or an inferiority complex.

Science can study the laws of suggestion which have been involved in our cure.

Faith consists in thanking God for our deliverance, and attaching ourselves to him. And impiety consists in taking advantage of our feeling of increased strength in life by throwing our weight about.

(*The Person Reborn*, 43)

Our world

The world is like a great ship on which we are all embarked without having wished to be so, and which, from time immemorial, has been disabled. In the beginning, through disobeying the captain's orders, the crew handled the ship badly, and it was holed. Since then, urged on by the instinct of self-preservation, or sometimes by a noble ideal, the crew has been feverishly trying to repair the damage. But the very fever, fear and confusion that reign create tumult, and the ship is handled worse than ever, so that even constructive efforts result in further damage. The sailors argue about the best method of effecting the repairs, and these arguments add to the disorder and confusion; the noise of them makes it impossible to hear clearly the captain's orders.

In this ship, each one is a victim, a victim of the fateful diabolical chain of events, a victim of the wrongs of others but each is at fault also, and contributes, even with good intentions, his share to the general tumult, to the bad handling of the ship, and to the panic. And the disaster which threatens each one is bound up with all the disorder. Each feels his responsibility since each must strive to avert it, and yet none can be judged to be more responsible than another.

(*A Doctor's Casebook*, 190)

The tragedy of our Western world is that it remains impregnated with Christianity, but has in general ceased really believing in it. The same man, for example, who declares that it is not possible to be honest in business, scolds his son sharply if he catches him in a lie. If we were frankly pagan we should be – perhaps – more immoral, but we should be less sick. The reason why there are so many sick is that this dichotomy in our Western civilization is reflected in the minds of all our contemporaries. Any inner cleavage between two contradictory tendencies gives rise to psychological troubles. There are always two ways of resolving an intrapsychic conflict, which is like disequilibrium in a balance. To overload the side that is too light is what the psychologists call overcompensation – the erection of a whole façade of virtue, morality and respectability, which is intended to hide from oneself and others one's inner malaise and shame. But to lighten the side that is too heavy is Christian sacrifice, the honest recognition of one's own sin in order to take it to God so as to be forgiven and set free.

This giving up of sin is also a reversal, a change of direction, in that the mind, instead of proceeding from the outside inward, in order to bring everything into itself, assessing every event according to the good it can extract, or the harm it might do itself, proceeds from the inside outward in order to forget itself and assess everything according to what it can give of itself to others.

(*The Person Reborn*, 130)

Formerly, man was controlled by social class: the family, the indissolubility of the marital bonds plus the filial respect imposed by tradition, the intimacy reigning in the craftsman's shop, the homogeneity of the trade guild, the cohesiveness of the city, and especially the community of faith and of moral, spiritual and social ideas brought about by the church – all these gave a framework to individual life. I do not pretend that man was any better, that he was, for example, in his heart any more faithful to his wife because public opinion did not allow him divorce! But a community of ideas bound him to the society of which he was a part. Today, on the other hand, he is lost in the anonymity of the large city and of big business. He is tossed to and fro by the most contradictory ideologies and dazzled by a popularized science that brings him more illusions than knowledge. Left alone to make the most perilous of intellectual experiments – that of developing his own philosophy of life — he lacks the necessary cultural means. He is the victim of a confusion never before known in his history, and he feels himself to be alone. Speak to him of the family, and he will answer 'outworn traditions'. Speak to him of the native land, and you will get 'exploitation of the people'.

(*Escape from Loneliness*, 20)

If we open our eyes upon those around us and upon ourselves, we see the game in which all, without exception, are engaged. Each plays what trumps he has to gain his own altruistic or egotistical ends. We are like chess-players scheming to win our game; or rather each of us lives his life like those chess-masters who play a hundred games simultaneously.

Whatever our aim – the conquest of a woman, of money, pleasure, esteem or notoriety, the defence of ourselves or our loved ones, or even of our opinions and our faith – moment by moment our attitudes and our words are governed by it and our personage moulded by it. It happens in every office, in every factory, in every society, in every committee, and even within the family circle. The assertive ones use the weapon of intimidation; others play on the heart-strings, or resort to cunning. Alliances are formed and dissolved, plans for revenge are made. A witty reply affords a way of escape; what we say very often serves less to express an opinion than to win a point or to justify ourselves.

(*The Meaning of Persons*, 30f.)

Each generation of pupils passes on to the next its store of 'tips' on how to answer the various masters in the examinations; for the aim is not to give vent to personal views, but to obtain the examination certificates which are the passport into a place in society. Later we learn the sort of behaviour which will win us acceptance among our workmates, the esteem of our chief, the respect of our rivals, the appreciation of our clients, and which will hold at arm's length those whose company would harm us, while helping us to associate with those who are useful to us.

The whole of our education, our titles, honours and decorations, our daily experience of life, our relationships, friendships, relatives, possessions, all go to make up our personage; they impart to it its peculiar physiognomy, and either consolidate or compromise our relations with everyone we meet. We have learned our lesson so well that it becomes as spontaneous as a new instinct. In order to see the unadulterated self it would be necessary to strip off all these accretions. But that is an illusion: if I burnt my diploma it would not stop anyone thinking of me as Dr Tournier. If I burnt all my books, I should still be the man who wrote them. (*The Meaning of Persons*, 33)

Each of us, to be sure, believes he is only defending sacred principles such as truth, fairness and reason. It is only in others that we discern self-interest, passion and sophism leading them on. This is why discussion so rarely can convince anyone. In all my life I can remember only one argument which really changed my mind. Political men know this, for they count far more on the power of suggestion in a few well-hammered slogans than in any rational argumentation.

Yet everyone continues unceasingly to argue, to put forth his logical reasonings which by-pass those of others to no avail. What joy people get when they discover some line of argument which appears irrefutable. They arouse the applause of their partisans who see in them already a decisive victory. But they are always disappointed and angered by the opponent's reaction, because a knock-out argument stimulates his ability to parry and awakens in him an abundance of arguments for the contrary. These are even more vigorous, which he in turn brandishes triumphantly, with no thought of refuting the argument just put to him.

(*To Resist or to Surrender*, 18f.)

Reason in no way directs men as it used to be believed. The analyses of historians, economists, Marxists, existentialists and psychoanalysts have for ever cured us of that illusion. Reason serves only to justify, within the field of full consciousness, the behaviour which obscure natural forces dictate to us, forces such as the instinct of preservation, of possession or of aggressiveness, of sexual desire, or of the instincts for power or for fulfilment.

(*To Resist or to Surrender*, 19)

Contempt in all its forms is extremely harmful and inhibiting. There are, of course, many shades and gradations of contempt, ranging in a subtle gamut from haughty disdain to secret scorn. It is not perhaps always open brutal contempt that is the most harmful, since it arouses in its victim a powerful defensive reaction. Such contempt is, for example, that felt by the Jew in an anti-Semitic environment, by the Negro in a segregationist society, by a businessman who has gone bankrupt in a capitalist system, or the illegitimate child surrounded by middle-class respectability.

But there are many lesser and more subtle forms of contempt, which slowly weigh down those on whom they fall, without exposing their flank to an active riposte. There is the mischievous little girl, bright and pretty, who teases her plain clumsy sister. Or the girl who pretends to be a little saint and so gets all the praise from her parents, and shames her more rumbustious sister. There is the big, tough boy who teases his weaker comrade because he cries instead of standing up for himself. There is the husband who lives with his wife almost as if she did not exist, except in brief moments of sexual intimacy. She does not even know whether he is listening when she speaks, and when she insists he shrugs his shoulders as if she were incapable of saying anything sensible. There is the pity shown by charitable people towards those less fortunate than themselves. Their zeal is sincere, but it is humiliating to those who are the objects of their generosity – they never talk to their equals in the tone of voice they use towards them.

(*Learning to Grow Old*, 55f.)

Modern man's loneliness is not the mark of those defeated in life, the sensitive or the nervous only, but equally of the leaders, of the elite.

We have so effectively preached a 'sincerity' in personal convictions that the most devoted people hold themselves back from the crowd and no longer find any community with which they can fully associate themselves. There is always a doctrinal or practical matter to which they cannot sincerely subscribe. They are repulsed by all mass movements and by everything that might be propaganda, and leave these in the hands of shallower minds. This is the great divorce between the elite and the people.

(*Escape from Loneliness*, 22)

The separation of thought from life has its roots deep within us, for we have become accustomed to distinguish between our belief and our behaviour. So effective is the distinction made that we no longer see how contradictory the two have become. To regain consciousness of this contradiction is to experience the conviction of sin, which in turn re-establishes the unity of knowledge and action. This is the condition that must be met if our political and social debates are to become a mutual, loyal and creative search, a search that unites us rather than a dispute that ever divides and pits us against one another. It is generally believed that political opponents are divided by questions of principle. Actually, the most bitter opponents are brothers at war, and that which divides them is emotional hostility, jealousy, grudge and pride.

(*Escape from Loneliness*, 166)

Father Raymond tells the charming story of a little child whose mother was teaching him to pray. When he got to the part, 'Lord, I surrender everything to thee, everything I own', he abruptly broke off and whispered to himself, 'except my baby rabbit'.

All of us have our baby rabbits. Sometimes it is an ugly thing, sometimes beautiful, sometimes large, sometimes small; but we are more attached to it than to anything else. But this is the thing that God asks of us and that he touches upon when we sincerely ask guidance of him. God does not, however, ask us to seek out our neighbour's little rabbits. Those who are greedy only in spirit condemn the love of money in others, and those who thirst only for glory condemn the base sensualism of the gay set.

(*Escape from Loneliness*, 111f.)

I think we often fail to do justice to people who are caught up in this frantic scramble for money and all that it can procure. We see in it nothing but selfishness, greed and lust for pleasure. Of course I know that men are selfish, but all men are equally so – those who look for cultural and spiritual satisfaction quite as much as those who go after material goods. In both types much more is involved than the mere desire for pleasure described by the Freudians. There is a need for fulfilment that is part of the stuff of life itself, a need for personal adventure which is peculiar to man, a thirst for the absolute, which in the last analysis is an expression of man's hunger and thirst after God.

(*The Adventure of Living*, 9)

The value of a human life does not lie in the 'rights of man', a fundamental concept of modern individualism, but in the spiritual bond that binds and subordinates him to his God and to his fellow men. It is the spirit which harmonizes the person and puts him in tune with himself. It is the spirit which also harmonizes society. This is why the problem of the 'moral person' and that of society are really one and the same problem.

The concept of the 'rights of man' presupposes that man is autonomous, and that he has value in his own right and not by virtue of the spirit he receives from above. It looks upon him as being capable of making a success of life through his own unaided efforts, of organizing society armed only with his intelligence and his technological skill. We see where that has led him.

We are like a child who has been given a beautiful mechanical toy as a Christmas present. His father says to him: 'Come along, and I'll show you how to make it go.' The child replies: 'No, I want to do it myself!' He tries, gets angry and sulky, takes it to pieces, damages it, and finally admits his incompetence. Defeated, he hands it to his father saying: 'There, you make it work.'

We too have received a beautiful and very complicated toy: life. We try to make it work on our own. We think we are having some success; but then things begin to go wrong, and we run into personal or social disasters. The more we struggle to put things right with our own strength, the worse does the situation become, until at last we come back to God, and offering our lives to him, say: 'Take over; I can't manage it on my own.'

(*The Person Reborn*, 201)

Self-discovery

The real meaning of travel, like that of a conversation by the fireside, is the disovery of oneself through contact with other people, and its condition is self-commitment in that dialogue. Those old Greek gods are not just poetry and legend. In them the Ancients personified living realities – intelligence, beauty, love or lust, which are still at work in our hearts, and which fashion our person. The language they speak is that of image and myth, which touches the person much more directly than the explicit language of science and the intellectual dialectic of the modern world.

It is also the language of the Bible, of the parables of Christ, which the rationalist of today finds it so difficult to understand, of the Word of God which demands of us not a discussion but a personal decision. Again, it is the language of the human heart, when it casts off the intellectualism in which it has been trained at school, and recovers its pristine freshness. It is the language of our dreams.

(*The Meaning of Persons*, 132)

I sometimes wonder whether the relationship of people with places is not more stable than that with their fellow human beings. For instance, we often find it difficult to remember a face, even if it is someone we have known well and loved. The face may come into our dreams with all the clarity of a photograph, whereas in the waking state we can summon up only a vague and imprecise picture of it. But when, on the other hand, a person is telling me the story of his life, he readily gives me a precise and detailed description of the various places which form the background of his experiences.

All our experiences, emotions and feelings are indissolubly linked in our memories with places. 'There are places we admire,' wrote La Bruyère, 'and there are others which affect us, and in which we should like to live. It seems to me that we depend on places for our thoughts, humours, passions, tastes and sentiments.' Man is not a pure spirit, and he has part in the places in which he has lived and experienced joy or sadness. He is bound up with matter, with things, with the ground he lives on. Our place is our link with the world. All the places we have lived in remain with us, like the pegs in a vast storehouse, on which our memories are hung. They symbolize all the states of mind through which we have lived, with all their varied shades of feeling.

(*A Place for You*, 14)

Often I see people who are obsessed with the search for a quite personal originality. They want to be really themselves, to break away from all the determining factors of their bodies, their heredity, their complexes, reflexes and upbringing. They resist every external influence, for fear of losing their personality. They want to owe nothing to anyone, have only original thoughts and feelings which no one has experienced before.

In the result, however, this turning in upon themselves, depriving them of fruitful intercourse with other people, impoverishes their lives and their personalities. What is left of us if we take away everything borrowed from outside and everything that partakes of the nature of habit within us? A gaping void. I once put it to one of these people like this: we do not do embroidery in the empty air, but on a piece of material. This material is like the network of automatisms, without which there would be no being, no life, no possibility of embroidery – that is to say, of personal creative activity.

(*The Meaning of Persons*, 95f.)

The whole of art, however personal it seems or tries to seem, is essentially communion, a bond between persons, a supra-personal and inter-personal reality. Cartesians always affirm the primacy of reason, the language of which they hold to be universal. But the language of images, of poetry and art, is universal also. There is no drama without convention, no photography even, without social convention. My dog does not recognize his photograph – to him it is only a blackened piece of paper.

The case of the ultra-modern artist is no different; his genius goes more or less against the conventions of his day, and therefore wins only tardy recognition; but he is helping to form new conventions. He succeeds in this because his genius is less original than it seemed, and awakens common echoes in the human heart. If he could be absolutely personal, he would remain absolutely alone, and he would not be an artist. In music our generation has witnessed an unparalleled revolution. I have seen a large number of young people whose parents disapproved violently of their addiction to jazz, even describing them as degenerate. I belong to the parents' generation, and it was only after these young people had confided intimately to me what the new music meant to them that I found that it had the power to awaken in me also secret echoes whose presence I had not suspected.

(*The Meaning of Persons*, 74)

Man before God

Many people are in fact even without being exactly aware of it, in dialogue with God: every time that their scale of values is called in question in the inner struggle, every time a man makes a reference to a standard of beauty, goodness and truth.

Man differs from the animals in that he asks himself questions. He asks them about the world and about himself, about the meaning of things, the meaning of disease and healing, life and death. He is conscious of his weakness, of his responsibility and of his short-comings, and he asks himself if there is any way out. I know that it is in fact God who puts these questions to him, that it is God who is speaking to him, even though he may not realize it. Faith consists only in recognizing who it is who speaks.

(*The Meaning of Persons,* 160f.)

A man's true value consists in his likeness to God. What gives value to his thoughts, his feelings and his actions, is the extent to which they are inspired by God, the extent to which they express the thought, the will and the acts of God. Sometimes, it is God's power which is manifested in a man's courage, in the authority with which he speaks and the strength with which he acts. But sometimes, also, it is God's tenderness which we observe in the heart of one who is weak, his creative suffering that we discover in a tormented soul. Remember the experience of Elijah, that giant of action, when, broken and discouraged in the desert, he understood that God was speaking to him in the still, small voice, rather than in the storm.

(*The Strong and the Weak*, 163)

We can have a more exact awareness of meeting God when there bursts forth in our minds some thought that imposes itself upon us by its authority, by its unmistakable savour of truth, a thought that transforms us, changes our attitude towards our problems, even if they are not solved on the intellectual plane. It is not the problems that change, but we ourselves; we evolve, and then the problems present themselves to us differently. What formerly revolted us is now seen as one of the great secrets of life, as a mysterious law of life. And at the same time we realize that the truth we have discovered not only is true for us, and for believers, but has a universal value; it helps us to understand ourselves, to understand all men, to understand life.

(*The Adventure of Living*, 147)

The true meaning of a religious experience does not lie in the transformation it effects in our lives, but in the fact that in it we have known God. That is what is lasting, even if our life remains a mixture of the divine and the human. That is what helps us to accept the drama of human life, which results from the very fact of the unending conflict in us between the divine and the human. It is indeed to the extent to which our experience has borne real fruit, to the extent to which our lives and our natures have undergone palpable, manifest change, that we can witness to the power of God. But that power goes far beyond our puny witness. What matters is not our experiences, but the fact that in them we have known the power of God's grace. That is a thing we do not forget, even if the day must come when the weaknesses, temptations and sins from which we had thought ourselves finally delivered reappear on the horizon; even if we must tirelessly battle on against our nature.

That is our task, to battle on, to hold our own against our inborn tendencies to strong or weak reactions, which we were given when we were given life itself, and which will be with us as long as we live. But the battle will not be the same as it was before. The faith born in us as the result of a concrete religious experience, survives even if we backslide. What is radically changed is the climate of our lives. Though our innate tendencies will remain with us, we shall on the other hand find it possible to break out of the vicious circles I have described, which constantly exacerbate those tendencies. Then if we still discover in ourselves, to our dismay, strong or weak natural reactions, far from being discouraged, we shall see them as opportunities for new deliverances.

(*The Strong and the Weak*, 248)

The Gospel does not condemn love of oneself; it only requires us to love others as ourselves; it asserts the value of the human person as being the creation of God. To esteem oneself as such, while at the same time frankly recognizing one's sinfulness, is the essential precondition of the experience of God's grace.

(*The Strong and the Weak*, 63)

The condition on which man receives the supernatural power of the Holy Spirit is his submission to the will of God. And it is quite clear that insofar as a man allows himself to be ruled by God in the use he makes of his strength, he can also deploy it without himself being afraid of it. Christianity does not, therefore, teach a doctrine of weakness. But the strength it gives a man is quite different from his natural strength. It is a God-directed strength, doing what God wills. It wins great victories, but they are only over evil and self, not the destructive victories that are won over others.

(*The Strong and the Weak*, 237)

Our attitude to life is always a reflection of our attitude to God. Saying 'Yes' to God is saying 'Yes' to life, to all its problems and difficulties – 'Yes' instead of 'No', an attitude of adventure instead of one of going on strike. In such an adventure we commit our entire being. It is not an escape. It is not obscurantism. We do not have to give up our reason, our intelligence, our knowledge, our faculty to judge, nor our emotions, our likes, our desires, our instincts, our conscious and unconscious aspirations, but rather to place them all in God's hands, so that he may direct, stimulate, fertilize, develop and use them.

(*The Adventure of Living*, 196)

God manifests himself in his works, expresses himself in them, reveals himself in them. They are not independent of him like things one produces and then abandons when they are completed. They remain in him, and he in them; they are in his hand and continue showing forth his presence. In this sense one can say that the Bible is existentialist. Never once does it present God as a philosophical concept, an abstract essence, an unexpressed potential. God is what he has done, what he does. His power is his creative acts, his goodness is his acts of goodness, his justice is his acts of justice. God's adventure is God himself, God who manifests himself, who manifests his life. So the fruit ripening on the tree manifests its life.

(*The Adventure of Living*, 86)

In this world, our task is not so much to avoid mistakes, as to be fruitful. To be more and more able to recognize our faults, so as the better to be able to understand the price of God's mercy, and to devote ourselves more completely to him, makes our lives more fertile. But to become obsessed with the effort to recognize our faults, and to refuse to act for fear of committing some sin, makes them sterile. Our vocation is, I believe, to build good out of evil. For if we try to build good out of good, we are in danger of running out of raw material.

(*The Person Reborn*, 80)

The quicker we are to discover our secret faults, the more do we need, if we are to avoid becoming obsessed by them, to understand the immensity of God's forgiveness. He asks us to recognize them, and humbly to turn away from them, solely in order for us to understand our poverty and his mercy, not so that we shall carry on in the utopian hope that we can ever act without sin entering into our action. 'When we are in doubt as to whether we have offended God,' says St Francis de Sales, 'we must humble ourselves, request God to excuse us, and ask for more enlightenment for another time, and forget completely what has happened and return to our accustomed way. For an inquisitive and anxious search to know whether we have acted rightly, indubitably arises from self-love.'

(*The Person Reborn*, 80)

Prayer

What we need is to rediscover an austerity of life and a solid piety which spring spontaneously from the conversion of the heart instead of being a formal constraint. All those people weighed down by the obsessive fear of 'doing something wrong', or who utter so many prayers that their very number suggests that the utterer has his doubts about their being heard, are not a very good advertisement for the way of God.

(*The Person Reborn,* 82f.)

The first requirement of religion is that we accept the laws of life. The spiritual life consists only in a series of new births. There must be new flowerings, new prophets, new adventures – always new adventures – if the heart of man, albeit in fits and starts, is to go on beating.

(*The Adventure of Living,* 39)

Prayer will not deliver us from our natural reactions, whether weak or strong; but it will bring us to recognize them for what they are, and thus continually to fresh experiences of grace.

(*The Strong and the Weak,* 150)

Do not let it be imagined that one must remain silent about one's feelings of rebellion in order to enter into dialogue with God. Quite the opposite is the truth: it is precisely when one expresses them that a dialogue of truth begins. I am reminded of the circumstances which one of my closest friendships began. It was a man I scarcely knew. A little younger than I, he had just joined a student's society of which I was a member. We had both been appointed delegates of our branch to a conference of the Berne branch. We had arrived too soon, and were sitting for a while on the banks of the Aar. We were engaging in a trivial conversation, which he suddenly interrupted with a direct question to me: 'Now tell me what it is you have against me.'

Thus a personal relationship with God which is to lead to the closest intimacy may sometimes begin from a stormy explanation. A man who thought himself an unbeliever suddenly sees that he was holding aloof from God because his heart was full of complaints against him, holding him responsible for his misfortunes. By giving expression to his reproaches he becomes more sincere – and the dialogue can begin.

(*The Meaning of Persons*, 164)

People often say to me: 'I don't seem to be able to say my prayers; what ought I to do?' I reply: 'Talk to God as you are talking to me; even more simply, in fact.' St Paul writes that the truest prayer is sometimes a sigh. A sigh can say more than could be contained in many words. We must be careful therefore not to restrict the living and spontaneous reality of prayer within some rigid formula.

(*The Meaning of Persons*, 165f.)

Countless writings underline the urgency for our modern world, with all its bustle and noise, of rediscovering the value of meditation, of silence, of prayer, of devotion. I preached it before I practised it. If one is to help the world towards this rediscovery, one must practise it oneself. The religious life must be fed. We devote years to studying a trade or profession. Ought we to show less perseverance in acquiring the experience of God? The least player of billiards or chess knows how long he has had to spend in order to learn to play, and how many games he had to lose before winning one. The scientist, when an experiment fails, instead of abandoning it, asks himself whether there has not slipped into his arrangements or his calculations some cause of error. One of my patients had a dream. She was given the task of keeping alight the fire under the boiler. A voice kept saying to her: 'Put coal on regularly. Don't let the fire go out.' Recently I saw a young woman who after several years of great spiritual adventure, was swamped in overwhelming difficulties. I happened to mention to her that during the last twelve years, I could count the days on which I had neglected to write down during meditation what I thought God expected of me. A few days later she wrote to me: 'I am grateful for what you said. It is a long time since I gave up the habit of written meditation. Someone told me that after a time one had made sufficient spiritual progress to be able to keep contact with God all day long, without having to reserve any special time for listening to him!'

Everything is habit in biology, and habits are created only by means of repetition. Experiments have shown how much of our behaviour is determined by the mental images to which our minds are constantly returning. If we bring our minds back again and again to God, we shall by the same inevitable law be gradually giving the central place to God, not only in our inner selves, but also in our practical everyday lives.

(*The Person Reborn,* 178f.)

I read in the newspaper an anecdote that goes very deep. A literary lady was holding forth in her drawing room, deploring the fact that she had not yet been touched by God's grace. 'How is one to believe that God exists?' she demanded. If he existed, would she not have had some answer out of him in the twenty-five years she had been addressing her requests to him? 'Pardon, Madame,' remarked one of her guests, 'but did you ever leave him time to get a word in?'

(*The Person Reborn,* 179)

There may be occasions where it would be more sincere not to indulge in meditation at all. I have seen several people give it up after having regularly practised it for long periods. I have never scolded them or urged upon them that it was their duty to take it up again as a matter of discipline. Instead I have tried to understand the spiritual development taking place within them. They were giving up their meditation because they were disappointed in its quality. It had become a hollow and unprofitable habit, an effort to find fine phrases that did not come from the heart, or a mere imitation of someone else. And sometimes I have seen them come back to it with fresh life and in a quite new and personal way. One man, of an essentially artistic or mystical temperament, tries to practise a kind of meditation that might be all right for someone else, but is far too intellectual for him. God does not speak only in terms of logical ideas, but also in pictures and music. Another perceives that his preconceived ideas about God, inculcated in him by others, are restricting his inspiration to far too narrow a field.

We have to rediscover periodically the meaning of living meditation. We realize that little by little, as a friend of mine once put it, we have taken to listening to ourselves instead of God.

(*The Person Reborn*, 183)

Many of the people I see yearn for a stable spiritual life. They blame themselves, after bursts of fervour, for falling back into lukewarmness, and after victories of obedience, for backsliding into sin. In this they are doubtless right – and I blame myself for the same thing; but I must at the same time bring them to see that that is our normal human condition. There is scarcely any such thing as a stable spiritual life. In any case it is rather a Hindu than a Christian ideal – the disappearance of the person, absorbed into the great Whole.

We do not 'possess' God, or contact with him. We find him periodically, and that is precisely the authentic and living religious experience. It is an adventure, of which the return of the Prodigal is an illustration, whereas the elder son, to whom the Father says 'Thou art ever with me' (Luke 15.31), undergoes no religious experience.

God has allowed man a greater margin of liberty than the animals. It is not only the organic margin of deviation of which we have spoken, and which by its fluctuations maintains the life of the body; it is a margin of moral disobedience which maintains, if I may put it so, his spiritual life.

(*The Meaning of Persons*, 114f.)

Complete sincerity is an unattainable ideal. But what *is* attainable is the periodic moment of sincerity, the moment, in fact, when we confess that we are not as we have sought to appear; and it is at those moments that we find contact with God once more.

The progress of our spiritual life is made up of these successive discoveries, in which we perceive that we have turned away from God instead of going towards him. That is what makes a great saint like St Francis of Assisi declare himself chief among sinners. We cannot, indeed, be content with this fluctuating condition, any more than we can resign ourselves to always rediscovering discordances between our personage and our person. We hear Christ's command: 'Be ye therefore perfect, even as your Father which is in heaven is perfect' (Matthew 5.48). We find this intuitive aspiration towards perfection in unbelievers as well as in believers. It implies especially a complete concordance between personage and person. Now it is precisely because we feel the impossibility of following this call that we recognize our need of God and his grace, of Jesus Christ and his atonement. If we thought we did not need God, should we still have a spiritual life?

This spiritual life, in its characteristic sudden creative welling up, is therefore entirely subjective, inexpressible and also intermittent. It is not manifested in the order of objectively observable phenomena except by its fruits: 'By their fruits ye shall know them' (Matthew 7.20). Now, these fruits are actually new automatisms, substituted for the old ones. St Paul enumerates them: 'The fruit of the Spirit is love, joy, peace, longsuffering, gentleness, goodness, faith, meekness, temperance' (Galatians 5.22–23).

(*The Meaning of Persons*, 115f.)

A fruit is a living thing. At the moment when the breath of the Spirit blows, all these qualities enumerated by the apostle well up like a spring of fresh water. But, inevitably, they gradually crystallize into new automatisms, and form a new personage. Thus piety is manifested in all the habits which go to make up this personage: regular prayer, confession, Bible-reading, the church with all its rites and ceremonies. He who, on a plea of preserving spontaneity, refuses to submit to any religious discipline, will find his piety becoming extinguished. Just as we were unable to grasp life apart from the automatic living phenomena of the body and the mind, so we cannot conceive of spiritual life detached from all concrete and regular expression.

These automatisms are the necessary servants of the spiritual life whose support they are. The oft-repeated prayer, learnt in childhood, is a habit of the mind, an indispensable aid to the expression of our spiritual life. It is no more possible to detach such automatisms from the spiritual life they serve than to separate the personage from the person. Their repetition has stamped us with the ecclesiastical forms among which our religious life has developed, and to alter its rites is to endanger that life itself.

(*The Meaning of Persons*, 116)

From time to time God raises up saints or prophets – a St Francis of Assisi, a St Bernard, a Wesley. From their personal experience a renewal of life flows out, new forms of piety and obedience, a new language which helps those who were beginning to lose them to understand the eternal verities of the gospel. Little by little these forms and this language establish their own tradition, becoming sacrosant formulae which will be broken down in their turn when there comes a new prophetic message.

Thus, in the spiritual life too, automatisms, the necessary servants of life, are at the same time its tomb. These habits of piety, indispensable as I have shown them to be, can very quickly become emptied of their truly creative substance, to become nothing more than the cloak of a devout personage. There are bigoted stick-in-the-muds in every church. In a pious family it is easy to mistake for a living faith what is in reality only a system of rigid principles which imprison life.

(*The Meaning of Persons*, 117f.)

There are moments of silent adoration which constitute supreme fellowship with God, a dialogue, even though it may not be put into thoughts and sentences. There are sudden moments of joy that are more binding than promises. There are heart-rending cries that ring truer than praises learnt by rote. There are liturgical prayers, repeated since childhood, into which one so puts one's heart that they are more personal than extempore prayers that strain after originality. Our own personal experience can never be taken as the norm for other people. What matters is that our prayers should be living and sincere. Each of us has his own temperament; one is more intuitive, another more logical; one is more intellectual, another more emotional. The relationship of each with God will be marked with the stamp of his own particular temperament.

(*The Meaning of Persons*, 166)

God's purpose

What characterizes the living being is neither its composition nor the physical and chemical phenomena which take place within it, but rather the fact that they are directed and organized. We could liken the living being to an orchestra directed by an invisible conductor. The scientist studying the orchestra and analysing each musician, can never succeed in bringing to light the secret of the harmony which results from their activity, since it is pre-established by the composer, and executed by the invisible conductor who alone knows the goal he aims at. Two wills are involved: the first is the composer who has established his plan; the second is the conductor who more or less faithfully interprets the first; the orchestra is a visible reality which to a greater or less extent obeys these two wills.

(*The Meaning of Persons*, 90)

God guides us, despite our uncertainties and our vagueness, even through our failings and mistakes. He often starts us off to the left, only to bring us up in the end to the right; or else he brings us back to the right, after a long detour, because we started off by mistake to the left in the belief that we were obeying him. He leads us step by step, from event to event. Only afterwards, as we look back over the way we have come and reconsider certain important moments in our lives in the light of all that has followed them, or when we survey the whole progress of our lives, do we experience the feeling of having been led without knowing it, the feeling that God has mysteriously guided us.

It was he who made us meet this man, made us hear that remark, read that book, with all the decisive consequences they have had on our lives. We did not perhaps know it at the time. Time has had to elapse to enable us to see it. Thus, the disciples on the Emmaus road talked with Jesus without recognizing him (Luke 24.13–35). It was he who brought us up short by means of a dream which at first we did not understand, a serious illness, a strange hesitation, or a painful failure. It was he also who guided us by means of a success, and so opened up a new and unexpected horizon to us. Ah, that is the true answer to our perplexing problem of success and failure!

(*The Adventure of Living*, 192)

Whence come our most original and creative ideas? In general we have no notion. God guides us through our associations of ideas, and through the working of our unconscious. An artist may be in despair, seeking an inspiration, then suddenly execute a work which astonishes even himself a little, and which he receives as a gift from God. We spend a lot of time wondering what is worthwhile, we discuss it with our friends, we seek advice, we pray and mediate, we complain at finding it so hard to see clearly, and then we find ourselves involved in adventures we have never thought of, and we feel that the hand of God is in them! What is 'worthwhile' is the fact those very adventures, directed by God, even if we have not understood at once their whole significance.

(*The Adventure of Living*, 193)

We can see God's plan for us only if we get rid of all preconceived ideas about it, since they are likely to contain much more human prejudice than true inspiration. Then instead of asking ourselves, on the level of formal moralism, whether such and and such a decision is good or bad in itself, we can turn to an examination of the underlying motives for the decision. In moving thus from conventional moralism to true morality, we can see that an action is, in general, neither good nor bad in itself, but only in relation to the sentiments that inspire it. It is clear that this 'change of perspective' does not lead to moral relativism. On the contrary, it involves a much more exacting morality. For example, it often shows up so-called virtues as a cover-up for secret sins.

(*The Person Reborn*, 50)

God has a purpose: the entire Bible proclaims this. What matters is that his plan should be understood and fulfilled. So, in the light of the Bible, the problem is shifted on to new ground. The question is no longer whether one is succeeding or failing but whether one is fulfilling God's purpose or not, whether one is adventuring with him or against him. It is, of course, always a joyful thing to succeed. But the joy is very deceptive if it comes from the satisfaction of an ambition that is contrary to the will of God. And of course failure is still very painful; but the pain is fruitful if it is part of God's purpose. A failure, within God's purpose, is no longer really a failure. Thus the Cross, the supreme failure, is at the same time the supreme triumph of God, since it is the accomplishment of the purpose of salvation. This is the true answer to the painful discovery that it is not possible to establish a clear frontier between success and failure. What is success and what is failure? The answer of the Bible is, 'What is the will of God? Are you obeying him?'

(*The Adventure of Living*, 149)

God calls Amos (Amos 7.14–15), the insignificant herdsman following his flock. He takes him out of his limited automatic life and makes him a prophet before the people and the king. Self-contemplation would never have led Amos to discover his person. He reveals it as he answers God's call. Here once more we see the nature of life and of the person. They are not essences, but acts; not static, but dynamic.

Everywhere in the Bible we see men thus touched by the divine dialogue, so that they find their true dimension. Their stature increases, and bursts the seams of the cramped garment of the personage. We are here at the heart of the problem of the person. We can see why introspection failed. However carefully and candidly a man examines himself today, he will not find what God will awaken in him tomorrow. His person is not a fixed datum, but a potential, a development, a plan known to God, and he will lead him day by day towards its fulfilment.

(*The Meaning of Persons*, 174)

The Bible gives us a powerful picture of men guided by God. They are not men who make no mistakes or who claim to make no mistakes, but men who seek to listen to God and obey him. After many mistakes and acts of disobedience, humbled by disappointments and trembling before God, Moses found intimate fellowship with him, so that he was able to receive the Ten Commandments direct from God. If Abraham had not believed the order to sacrifice his son, would he have had the experience that was his at the moment when God stayed his arm from a sacrifice which so many other religions saw as the cruel will of the deity? And then there are all the prophets called by God, balking at the call they receive. 'If I say, "I will not mention him, or speak any more in his name",' says Jeremiah, 'there is in my heart as it were a burning fire shut up in my bones' (20.9). And there is St Peter, making his heartfelt remonstrations to Jesus when the latter announces that he is going to be put to death, and drawing upon himself the sharp reply: 'Get behind me, Satan! . . . for you are not on the side of God, but of men' (Matthew 16.23). And this was at the very moment when St Peter had just proclaimed, with the purest inspiration, his faith in the divinity of Christ. And there is the Church of Antioch receiving as it prayed the order to send Paul and Barnabas on a mission, and Paul himself 'led by the Spirit' when he comes back to Jerusalem, or seeing a dream in which a Macedonian calls him as God's command to take the gospel to Europe (Acts 16.9).

Christ himself is the incarnation of this life led in its smallest details by the Spirit. He walks peacefully, seeing in the man met on the road or the woman at the well the very soul to whom God has sent him. No rush, no concocted plan, no disorder; everything takes place in its own time, as he himself so often says. But this does not stop him from withdrawing with his disciples to seek God's guidance. He returns full of assurance, to go up to Jerusalem to face death.

All these men of the Bible accept God's precise orders – the place they must go to, the time they must go there. But they do not look for these orders as for oracles. What they seek is God. Following the *directions* they receive, they find their lives *directed* towards fellowship with God. They do not express their fellowship sentimentally, but manifest it through their faith in the concrete *directions* they are following.

(*The Person Reborn*, 193f.)

The Bible moves entirely in the perspective of a divine purpose and of a God who calls men to fulfil it, at the same time fulfilling their own personal destiny. Look at St Paul, the Pharisee, the doctor of the law, meticulously engaged in searching the Scriptures to find there the nature of God and of truth. Suddenly the dialogue breaks into being on the Damascus Road (Acts 9), and his life is transformed into an incredible adventure. He does not stop being a scholarly theologian, but he finds truth in action, fighting for Christ. In everything he writes we can hear the echo of the passionate dialogue in which he is daily engaged. He asks for deliverance from an affliction, and God's answer is: 'My grace is sufficient for you' (II Corinthians 12.9). He desires to retrace his steps towards Asia, towards the familiar churches, and God speaks to him in a vision; by the apparition of a Macedonian he calls him to go over into Europe (Acts 16.9).

Prayer constantly enlarges our horizon and our person. It draws us out of the narrow limits within which our habits, our past and our whole personage confine us. Sometimes we receive a clear command, whose implications we do not usually at first understand. It is only afterwards, as we look back over the road we have travelled, that we see that God had a purpose for us, and that he has compelled us to follow it in spite of ourselves.

The person is the divine plan of our life, the guiding force, itself directed by God, who leads us towards our vocation in spite of every deviation.

At some point on this journey we shall find that we have crossed a frontier: through personal fellowship with God we pass from the world of things to the world of persons.

(*The Meaning of Persons*, 175f.)

The men of the Bible who show us the road of faith obeyed without being able to be sure that they were not mistaken. So today, those who exercise a real apostolate are those who have taken not only moral, but also material risks. For a business-man this often means the prospect – humanly speaking – of failure. Those whose witness affects us most are not always the clergy, whose material security is guaranteed by the church, but men who live by faith and who demonstrate practically that God does not desert those who serve him, even if they are called upon to give up all material wealth and a regular income. Yet, let us be careful not to make a false distinction between those who are guided to give up all material security and the others. We must not confuse faith with optimism or the vanity of a sensational gesture. God calls each of us in secret to make certain sacrifices which always involve a risk, even though it may differ from person to person. God speaks to the crowd, but his call comes to individuals, and through their personal obedience he acts. He does not promise them nothing but success, or even final victory in this life. The goal of the adventure to which he commits them is in heaven. God does not promise that he will protect them from trials, from material cares, from sickness, from physical or moral suffering. He promises only that he will be with them in all these trials, and that he will sustain them if they remain faithful to him. The trials will then become the occasion for the renewal of the adventure, instead of for bitterness and rebellion.

(*The Person Reborn*, 231)

We must beware of attributing a magical value to God's guidance. Above all we must beware, wretched and blind as we are, of arguing with each other about it. Our basic attitude is what matters most: a sincere seeking after God's will. We must always respect that sincerity in others.

(*The Person Reborn*, 186)

Nothing is more futile than to argue endlessly about whether, on some occasion in the past, one has made a mistake or not.

I have an old friend, an excellent person, whose witness once helped me to see that the seeking of God's guidance is, despite all our mistakes, the surest rule of life. Caught up in the tragic events of the war, he found himself facing a serious decision. He prayed, he meditated with some friends. He made the choice that seemed to him to conform with God's will. But the course of events made him doubt whether he had made the right decision in his country's interest. He underwent an inner crisis. He came to spend a few days with me. Every morning we read the Bible together, before our meditation. On the last day we had read the story of Lot's wife, who was turned into a pillar of salt because she looked back (Genesis 19.26). Then my friend exclaimed 'I am like Lot's wife. My life is petrified because I keep looking back. I turn that old problem over and over in my mind, uselessly, without ever discovering whether I did right or not. My life is no longer an adventure, because my faith is shaken and I am not looking for God's guidance any more. I want to start going forward again.' Shortly afterwards a message from a friend who had died for his country finally relit in him the flame of dedication to Christ, and his life once more bore fruit. 'To will what God wills is the only science that gives us rest,' wrote Malherbe.

We all find it difficult to understand God's guidance, because we lack imagination. We are the prisoners of our prejudices. A colleague once remarked to me that we are always wanting to arrange everything, order everything, reconstruct everything. If we read the Old Testament prophets we see that sometimes, on the contrary, the will of God is that everything should be destroyed, that the cup of sin be drained to the dregs, so as to make possible a resurrection. We find it hard to understand the detours along which God takes us, and it is often only afterwards that we see that we had to go that way.

(*The Person Reborn*, 170)

Men may be mistaken in the goals towards which they strive in their adventures; they may be motivated by hate or a desire for revenge; they may be mistaken in the means they employ; but the force that impels them into all kinds of adventure, bad as well as good, is a divine gift, a sign of love. One only begins really to understand men when one sees that even in their worst errors they are moved by a desire to give themselves to something greater than themselves. When we realize this divine quality in our instinct of adventure, we feel our responsibility towards God to direct it in accordance with his loving will.

(*The Adventure of Living*, 93)

To seek the meaning of things and God's will does not spare us either from error or from doubt; nor does it resolve all the mysteries of our destiny, all the insoluble problems which are set us by any event in nature or in our lives; nevertheless, it does give a new meaning to our lives.

(*A Doctor's Casebook*, 37)

When I am the witness of a spiritual event, in which I see a man humbly coming back to God to dedicate himself to him, I am well aware that this is the result of an inner crisis determined by the influences to which he is subject, but I know also – and he feels it to be so – that God has brought him on purpose to this point, using the whole process of the events through which he has led him. Similarly, in the life of a nation it may seem to the observer who looks at history on the level of immediate cause and effect, that a certain event is the necessary consequence of the action of a certain man, and that it is itself the cause of another event which necessarily results from it. But if this process is viewed as a whole, there becomes apparent a line of evolution and a more general causality. A certain man or a certain event must play a part at a certain moment in history, in order that the destiny of that nation should be fulfilled. Such a destiny will be perceived by a vaster intuition.

(*The Person Reborn*, 27f.)

Jesus

For the Greeks everything was immutable. They had a static conception of the world.

The Jews conceived of God as intervening in history; hence they looked forward to a future golden age.

The Indian religions see this perfection as the end of a gradual process of spiritualization.

For the Christian all is accomplished in Jesus Christ. The centre of history, the decisive intervention of God, is behind us, and so we are delivered from the hopeless problem of how we are to scale the heights of heaven. Nevertheless we have an inborn feeling of our own perfectibility.

It seems to me that evolution, as presented to us by science, provides a useful illustration of this difficult question. At each stage of evolution – the appearance of life on the earth, for instance – a quite new fact intervenes, unexplained by the determining factors that have gone before. This new fact, however, will take many centuries to realize its many possibilities in all the multitude of increasingly differentiated living creatures that will make their appearance; and yet all those possibilities were already contained in the very first appearance of life.

In the same way Jesus Christ is a historical reality. He marks the beginning of a new stage, the reign of the Spirit. This reign was fully contained in its first appearance, but God incarnates it gradually in all these new appearances of the Spirit, as each of us experiences the reversal of his inner attitude, following in Christ's footsteps and receiving his grace.

(*The Person Reborn*, 134f.)

Into a world which witnessed the triumph of strength – at the time of the Roman Empire – and in which the weak were despised, Christ brought an incredible reversal of values, that which is expressed in the Beatitudes. He held out his hand to the weak, the sick, the poor, sinners – to all those upon whom society passed censure. But it was not only a revolution in concepts and ideas that Christ brought. At his touch, the sick were healed, the weak became strong, men who until then had been the slaves of their natural propensities were liberated from them. It was not only the rehabilitation of the weak, but their liberation; and not only the liberation of the weak, but also of the strong.

We may still see today men delivered from the chain of their natural reactions after experiencing the grace of God. We see sick people regain physical vitality; we see neurotics delivered from psychological inhibitions on which sometimes even the best treatment has had no effect. But we also see the strong becoming gentle; we see them throwing off the armour-plating which imprisons them, their armour of health, insensitiveness and self-confidence.

That is why concrete witness has always made a great impression on me.

(*The Strong and the Weak*, 208)

The housewife should not fail to note the passage in St John's Gospel (John 21.9) which shows us Jesus, shortly after his resurrection, roasting fish for his disciples over a coal-fire. We tend always to oppose the spiritual to the material; it is not thus that we should expect to see Christ, after his resurrection, and on the eve of his ascension, preparing for one of his last interviews with his disciples. Nevertheless, he chooses to show his love for them by this simple everyday act, like any mother preparing a meal for her husband and children.

(*A Doctor's Casebook*, 23)

No book on theology or ethics, no matter how inspired, can fill the immense gap between our finiteness and the undreamed-of greatness of God. Only Jesus closed the gap, but starting from the other end, by stripping off his divine majesty and putting on our human existence. Only he was able to know ever when to resist and when to surrender. Moreover, this demanded of him the utmost faithfulness in meditation, in fasting, in prayer. This is why Christianity is not so much a body of principles as it is a commitment to his person. By him, in fellowship with him, it is possible for us to receive certain benefits of grace, a few rays of light far more authentic and trustworthy than the whole store of human knowledge.

All we can do is try: try sincerely to live a life guided by God. If we want to be altogether sure of his guidance before beginning, we shall fall back into all the problems we have already described. He who does not dare risk being mistaken about the will of God will never come to know him any better. For it is through obedience, yes, even through our misguided actions, that we find even greater light. That is, on condition that we are willing to re-examine our actions afterwards quite honestly and as in the presence of God. God is ever the hidden one who reveals himself only through our groping after him.

(*To Resist or to Surrender*, 48f.)

Christian experience first of all restores the human person and then spreads out from person to person until it transforms society. Christ, after having preached to thousands, concentrated his attention upon a few disciples. It was to this handful of men that he confided the enormous task of taking his message to the ends of the earth. God's method throughout all of history has been one of personal calls. He calls a Moses or a Francis of Assisi, a Paul or a Karl Barth, to a life of rugged obedience, from which self-discipline all their spiritual, social and political ministry flows forth.

(*Escape from Loneliness*, 163)

God wills the development of all men. When from time to time he makes them hear his call to self-denial, to renunciation and even self-sacrifice, it is not for their impoverishment but for their enrichment. Christianity is in full accord with psychology. Like psychology, it sees man in continual evolution from a lesser condition to a greater one, from limited freedom to greater freedom, from poor wealth to truer wealth. The gospel of Jesus Christ is nothing if not a gospel of growth. It sets our eyes on a development more complete than any that can be conceived by a psychology confined within the limits of nature. All Christ's calls to detachment are accompanied by promises which point to their real meaning. In answer to the apostle Peter's question, he says: 'Every one who has left houses or brothers or sisters or father or mother or children or lands, for my name's sake, will receive a hundredfold, and inherit eternal life' (Matthew 19.29).

(*A Place for You*, 208)

There are two basic tendencies in the human mind: revolution and tradition – adventure and stability, boldness and prudence. Once again, let us be careful not to set them up as incompatible opposites. Each has its own riches – power, for the first, fidelity for the second. Each also has its own dangers – pride, for the first, idleness for the second. Only in Christ do we find both in perfect harmony. He stood firm against conventional respectability and set blowing the most powerful wind of revolutionary change that humanity could ever know. He breathed life into tradition, and restrained his disciples from any violent act of revolt.

(*The Person Reborn*, 211)

Attachment to the person of Christ means avoiding both moral dogmatism and moral anarchy. The reader will realize that all I have been saying against despotic dogmatism could well open the door to a no less dangerous individualism, subjectivism and amorality, if all we had to guide us was a moral code, instead of a living person. If man is not to look upon himself as a god, or a sovereign interpreter of God, he needs an objective criterion of truth: and this we have in Jesus Christ. We may do anything at all provided it is done with Christ. He alone frees us both from passive conformity and from rebellious nonconformity. If we think of him in every circumstance of our lives; consult him on every point; seek him in every person we meet; and whenever we are faced with a decision, ask ourselves what he would do; ask ourselves in every affliction and every blessing what he is saying to us in that affliction or that blessing; then we shall be passionately interested in everything and everybody; we shall take everything seriously but nothing tragically; we shall unify our lives and our personalities, through giving them one single axis. Above all we shall find ourselves daily taking the road that leads to the reversal of our attitude, which we can never achieve by ourselves.

(*The Person Reborn*, 132f.)

Jesus Christ has his own way of turning society upside down: the Cross. Instead of calling the hosts of heaven to defend him against the political and religious establishment which was harrying him, he conquered fear in himself. In the same way he leads those who give themselves to him to the inner reversal about which we have spoken, and which is the only way of resolving the dichotomy between adventure and love.

He calls us to a wonderful adventure, one that is creative and not destructive. Instead of an exhausting and fruitless crusade against the many-headed monster of external evil – of other people's sin – he calls us to an inner adventure, to a crusade against the evil in ourselves.

Instead of taking up arms against all the things around us that quite properly we find outrageous, he calls us to make war against the things we are ashamed of within ourselves. Instead of denouncing and attacking all the shortcomings of society, he calls us to recognize our own shortcomings so that we may become a healthy unit in society. The external battle fills our hearts with bitterness, criticism and rebellion; the internal battle liberates them and brings back a smile to our faces.

Rebellion is contagious, and when men are criticized and attacked they defend themselves and launch into criticism and attack in their turn. In the same way, inner liberation and a smiling face are also infectious, and when we put right our own wrongdoing, other people begin to look to theirs.

We are all closely bound up together. Every act or word helps to propagate either good or evil. If our neighbours' faults arouse our indignation and goad us to an aggressive reply, our attitude has in its turn the same effect on them, and the resulting chain of evil cause and evil effect can play havoc in a family, a workshop, or a whole country. On the other hand, if we recognize our own faults, our neighbours will also examine their own lives. If we trust them, they will trust us. If we try to understand them, they will try to understand us. In a combat group all that is needed is one soldier animated by a spirit of bitterness for the contentment and *esprit de corps* of the whole group to be undermined; but also the example of the self-sacrifice of one man is all that is needed for them to be restored.

Christ's method of changing the world is to use the spirit that radiates from a person who has experienced a change of heart.

(*The Person Reborn*, 212f.)

The Bible

The Bible is the book of adventure and must be read as such. Not only the adventure of the world and of humanity, but the personal adventure of each man and woman whom God touches, calls and sends into action. In it we find that coming together of adventure and poetry to which I referred in connection with myths and epics. Children feel this spontaneously, and hence in one sense we are to divest ourselves of our cold intellectualism and become children again. In the Bible we rediscover the deep emotion which rekindles in us the fire of adventure. The Bible also gives adventure its true meaning, for from end to end it reveals what is at stake in all our work, all our choices, and all our self-commitment.

(*The Adventure of Living*, 82)

The extreme realism of the Bible explains the contradictions which we find in it, and which are often very perplexing for us. The Bible is, in fact, a mirror of the human heart, and the human heart is full of contradictions; it never grasps more than a part of the truth, and that part it then generalizes as if it were absolute.

Thus St James tells us that temptation does not come from God (James 1.13), and yet in the Lord's Prayer Jesus teaches us to ask God not to lead us into it (Matthew 6.13). Similarly, numerous passages affirm that disease and death do not come from God, but from his enemy, from Satan, from the Devil (I Corinthians 15.26; Luke 13.16); and elsewhere it is written: 'If thou wilt not hearken unto the voice of the Lord thy God . . . the Lord shall smite thee with the boil of Egypt, and with the emerods and with the scurvy, and with the itch, whereof thou canst not be healed. The Lord shall smite thee with madness, and with blindness, and with astonishment of heart' (Deuteronomy 28.15, 27–8); and again: 'See now that I, even I, am he . . . I kill, and I make alive, I have wounded, and I heal' (Deuteronomy 32.39).

Let us not look in the Bible for logic, but for life; for logic is powerless to grasp and to express life.

(*A Doctor's Casebook*, 19)

It is in fact life that we find in the Bible, and not a system of thought. We know that there is something true and vital in each of those apparently contradictory affirmations, whereas no logical system would be true. A philosophical system necessarily juggles with the truth. We are nearly always longing for an easy religion, easy to understand and easy to follow; a religion with no mystery, no insoluble problems, no snags; a religion that would allow us to escape from our miserable human condition; a religion in which contact with God spares us all strife, all uncertainty, all suffering and all doubt, in short, a religion without the Cross. In the Bible, God does not take man out of his drama; but he lives it with him and for him. The Bible avoids nothing. It enters realistically into our life as it is. It expresses all our feelings, all our aspirations, all our fears and all our contradictory intuitions. On every page it utters the cries of human suffering, from the anguish expressed so poignantly by Job:

Why died I not from the womb?
Why did I not give up the ghost when I came out of the belly?
Why did the knees receive me?
Or why the breasts, that I should suck?
For now should I have lien down and been quiet;
I should have slept; then had I been at rest (Job 3.11–13)

to the agony of Christ on the Cross: 'My God, my God, why hast thou forsaken me?' (Matthew 27.46). On every page, too, it proclaims the certainties of faith: 'Fear thou not, for I am with you' (Isaiah 41.10).

The amazing wealth of the Bible is precisely what makes it a difficult book to study.

(*A Doctor's Casebook*, 19f.)

The Bible is not concerned to give precise definitions of such ideas as the spirit or the soul, or to set forth a systematic philosophy of the nature of man. It uses several different words in turn for one and the same reality such as the soul, and one and the same word may be used to mean successively things which we distinguish: the mind and the heart. It is more poetic, more intuitive, and above all more dynamic, than we are. It gives a picture of man living, moving, perpetually becoming, rather than a static image dissected into its component parts. Thus, that which man has received from God, that which makes him different from the animals, his spirituality, his mind, his soul, whatever name we give it, is not described in the Bible as a thing, a part of man, a substance, but as a breath, a movement, an impulse, an echo of God's voice.

(*A Doctor's Casebook*, 21f.)

There are two sorts of minds. The first is the superficial mind. For these people there is no mystery. They always know what to do. They are more ready to give advice than to listen to it, to understand, or to change their opinions. On the other hand there are those who possess the sense of mystery, who are conscious of the gaps in their knowledge and of its limits, for whom every sick person is an enigma that will never be completely explained. It is not the first who are the more scientific of the two.

But we all have in us these two tendencies. None of us can flatter himself that he has escaped the danger of the 'knowledge which puffeth up'. But we are protected from it by reading the Bible. However powerful and learned he may be, the Bible always sets man face to face with God, reminding him thus of his frailty and his weakness: 'Put no more trust in man, with his mere breath of life: of what account is he?' (Isaiah 2.22).

(*A Doctor's Casebook*, 28)

One is struck by the number of people, believers as well as unbelievers, who look in the Bible for just those passages which do not apply to them. Those who are tortured, crushed and in despair pick out the hard words that Jesus addressed to the smug Pharisees – the passages in which he speaks of God's judgment, of the sin against the Holy Ghost which will not be forgiven, or of the gates of heaven which are closed against those who arrive too late. Those who are optimistic, superficial and self-satisfied, however, pick out the words which Christ addressed to outcasts and sinners to assure them of God's forgiveness which blots out every sin.

(*The Person Reborn*, 129)

The Bible does not despise the body. It calls it the temple of the Holy Spirit (I Corinthians 6.19). 'I will give thanks unto thee; for I am fearfully and wonderfully made,' cries the psalmist (Psalm 139.14). The supreme witness of God's love – we may say, therefore, his most 'spiritual' act – the Bible sees to be in the incarnation of Jesus Christ, in his taking the 'likeness and fashion' of a man, with all the consequences that are involved, including suffering and death (Philippians 2.6–7). Elsewhere St Paul compares the love of a man for his wife with that of Christ for his church (Ephesians 5.25); and in the realism of the Bible that means an all-embracing love, carnal as well as spiritual. Similarly the physiological harmony of the body, the working together of all its organs, is presented as the image of the accord that should reign in the church through charity (I Corinthians 12.12–30). Thus, in the biblical perspective, God's purpose is manifested in the harmony of nature as well as in the spiritual communion of souls.

(*A Doctor's Casebook*, 58)

Why does the Bible so often speak of the 'living' God? Surely it is because the God it reveals to us is not the God of the philosophers, outside time and space, the origin of all things or the sublimest possible conception of the mind. He is a living person, a person whose voice breaks in upon us, who himself intervenes, who acts, who suffers, who enters into history in Jesus Christ, who enters into men by the Holy Spirit. We recognize in him the characteristics of life that we studied earlier – not so much motionless essence as movement, impulsion, guiding force.

At the same time the Bible reveals to us what the person is. Man is the being to whom God speaks, with whom he thus enters into a personal relationship. After having created the whole inorganic world, and all the plants and animals – a world blindly and impersonally subject to him – God created man in his image; that is to say, a personal being, a partner in dialogue, a being to whom he might speak and who could answer, to whom he gave liberty, and whose liberty, refusals and silences he respects, but whose replies he also awaits.

(*The Meaning of Persons*, 163)

Magic

There are two contrary errors: to refrain, for fear of magic, from every kind of bold and sensational act, even when God requires it of us; this course has been all too common in the church, and is what has made it as poor as it is today in manifestations of God's power. And, on the other hand, through zeal to demonstrate that power, to run after the sensational, even when God does not will it, and so fall into magic; certain religious sects are guilty of this. In the gospel, the sceptics sneered at the miracles of Galilee and at the cross: 'He saved others; let him save himself, if this is the Christ of God, his chosen' (Luke 23.35). Neither the miracles nor the cross can be taken out of the gospel without distorting it.

(*A Doctor's Casebook*, 116)

Take the woman who, in a moment of perplexity, opens her Bible at random, and happens to light upon a passage which exactly meets her need; she sees in it a direct personal message from God. She is in danger of magic if on another occasion she uses the same means and imagines that she is certain to find God's reply to her new problem in some verse thus chosen.

(*A Doctor's Casebook*, 118)

Belief in magic insinuates itself into our hearts, coming in the wake of even our most authentic spiritual experiences. It rears its head the moment we make generalizations based on a particular experience, as soon as we claim that that experience is the necessary condition that inevitably leads to true faith. We see that the indefinable frontier between faith and magic is the frontier between humility and pride, between the humble search for God and the proud claim to possess him. This is the psychological cause of all the quarrels that divide Christians. Such disputes are tragic and fruitless, for each invokes in support of his own system the living experience on which it was based, without seeing that between the experience and the system there has been a subtle switch from one wavelength to another, from faith to magic.

(*A Doctor's Casebook*, 118f.)

We often hear Protestants reproaching Catholicism for conferring a magical value on the sacraments, on the priesthood, on dogma, or on the church. But they are confusing the systematization with the authentic experience on which it is based, and from which too many Protestants are cut off by their fear of magic. The psychologist can see quite as many magical deviations – many of them less consciously realized – in Protestantism, where they abound among the various sects, among the pietist movements, and even among the rationalists, who do homage to the magic of Reason. The spirit of magic lies in wait for the Christians as much as for the agnostics and the pagans. It arises, in fact, from an inherent tendency in human nature, and none of us can boast of being proof against its wiles. It is the longing for the fairy tale, for the magic wand that will charm away the difficulties of life, the suffering, the limitations, and the uncertainties of our human condition.

(*A Doctor's Casebook*, 119)

Man finds himself in an impossible dilemma as long as he thinks he must choose either reason or magic and faith confused together: he has to repress one or the other of the two, to become either a rationalist, stifling his mystical longings, or a mystic, stifling the voice of his reason. The integration of his person, the harmonious marriage of his deductive and the inductive functions, is possible only if he accepts the true dilemma: the choice between magic and true faith, faith in the one true God.

It seems that the human mind is too small to grasp God in his fullness; so it clings to one of his attributes, one of his gifts, exaggerating its importance, and basing a system of life on it. The Bible, the church, dogma, experience, meditation, ceremonies, spiritual gifts or natural gifts – all have their true value, but we end up by claiming to confine God in them.

(*A Doctor's Casebook*, 120)

Dogmatism

The spirit of dogmatism ossifies thought and sterilizes life. The person who is satisfied with one experience loses the dissatisfaction which could be the source of fresh experiences.

I have had a close friendship with a group of French pastors who conducted evangelistic missions with wholehearted zeal in various parishes. After one of these, they were received, in the late evening, by one of the notables of the parish. The latter was expressing his enthusiasm for the spiritual message they had brought. He added: 'As a matter of fact, I too have had a religious experience.' And turning to his wife, he said: 'Would you mind going up to the attic and getting it? You remember I wrote it out and framed it. It must be in the big chest at the far end. These gentlemen would be interested to see it.' A moment later the wife came back with the famous religious experience under her arm, but she had to beg pardon for producing it in such a condition, because the rats had been at it and had left it in a lamentable state!

(*The Person Reborn*, 101)

Men are infinitely diverse. They travel along many different roads. There is always something new to be learned from each one, so long as one retains the spirit of seeking. But they are also diverse within. Several contradictory beings are at war within them, often without their knowledge, and their reactions are constantly overlapping. There are their father and mother, their forbears, something of all the teachers that have moulded them, and of all the influences to which they have been subjected. This explains why we can have so much sympathy for people whose ideas seem wrong to us, and so little for others who share our beliefs. While they are developing one thesis, there is in them a being who is representing the opposite thesis. If they talk a lot about the value of the community, that is because there is at work within them a strong tendency towards individualism against which they are defending themselves. Inner harmony is the aspiration of all.

The spirit of dogmatism simplifies, opposes and systematizes. The philosophical spirit has a sense of the endless complexity of things.

(*The Person Reborn*, 107)

The daily observation of men and women shows me that believers and unbelievers are much closer to one another than one would think if one judged by their dogmatic controversies. There are determinists who call themselves unbelievers on account of their scientific philosophy, but who have hearts of gold and use their determinist ideas to help them understand their fellow men; and so they act with gentle humility towards others while at the same time being extremely strict with themselves. There are hard-hearted orthodox believers who use their moral view of the world for little else than to hurl anathemas about, without observing their own faults. 'Not every one who says to me, "Lord, Lord,' shall enter the kingdom of heaven,' said Christ, 'but he who does the will of my Father who is in heaven' (Matthew 7.21).

(*The Person Reborn*, 127)

The proclamation of the truth, truly inspired by God and by love of our fellow men, is infinitely fruitful. But when it is inspired by a spirit of controversy and by personal motives, it divides the church and troubles men's minds. There are no more bitter controversialists than those new converts who criticize the errors of the church they have left, and the psychologist cannot but note the personal factors which underlie their ardour. For example, their conversion is often seen to be a projection of a revolt against their background, their upbringing, their parents and a whole mental outlook which has crushed them, and on which they are now taking revenge.

(*The Person Reborn*, 100)

Behind every system of thought there is a living experience. It would be easy to show this in the history of philosophy. Similarly, one can read the autobiography of an author in all the novels he writes. To set up one system or doctrine against another impoverishes the mind by freezing it in a partisan attitude which obstructs the evolution of its life. How many upholders of orthodoxy seem to have fossilized minds, through having lost that unquenchable disquiet and curiosity which are the precondition of every advance in the spiritual life! As soon as one believes one possesses the truth, and encases it in a system, one shuts out other horizons. The mind is so made that it cannot formulate any affirmation that does not also imply a negation. The individualist runs the risk of failing to appreciate the mystical reality of the community, which is no less important. In upholding the value of the community one runs the risk of failing to appreciate the incomparable value of the individual personality, the chosen ground of all decisive spiritual events. The believer runs the risk of failing to appreciate the riches of doubt and of scientific research. The sceptic runs the risk of not appreciating the incomparable power of faith.

(*The Person Reborn*, 106)

God alone can help us to build the unity of our lives in all their richness and complexity. For everything is contained in God, who gives each idea its meaning and its place in the whole complex of ideas. As long as we make these exclusive distinctions between them we shall go on shutting ourselves and others up in mental impasses. There is law in the gospel, and also grace; there is God's judgment as well as his forgiveness; there are the follies of faith and also the wisdom of prudent foresight; there is the cross and the resurrection. Our minds are too small ever to grasp more than one aspect of the truth at a time; and then they make artificial distinctions between the different aspects. Jesus Christ is the unique and total incarnation of truth, the only way, the only life, and yet we betray his spirit of love when we build a wall between Buddhists, Jews or Moslems and ourselves. He is our only Master, and yet without betraying him we can learn from the Greek philosophers, the sages of India, the philosophers of China or the sacred texts of ancient Egypt. And I see so many people torn in two between Catholicism and Protestantism! The more priests and pastors they consult, each denouncing the errors of the other's church, the more are they pushed into opposing the one to the other in their minds, thus sterilizing their spiritual life; and so the unity of the church, which Christ commanded, is in spirit destroyed. Also, many people are torn in two by the dichotomy between the doctrines of some sect or religious movement to which they have been attracted by its fervour, and those of the traditional church which denounces its errors but lacks its zeal. So many people are torn in two by the arguments of the theologians. Long ago Johann Tauler of Strasbourg wrote concerning the Trinity: 'Leave your arguments about it, but see to it that the Holy Trinity is within you.'

(*The Person Reborn*, 108f.)

Strength and weakness

'The exterior is the signature of the interior,' wrote Jacob Boehme. The reason why external events, such as unjust criticism, hurt us so much is that they find an echo in our own malaise. The person who has doubts about himself is extremely sensitive to the criticisms of others. The self-confident person does not even notice them. We are afraid of the external enemy because of the 'fifth column' we are aware of in ourselves. We are very ready to look upon external events as bolts from the blue which come to upset the normal course of our lives. The day comes when we look upon them as the necessary instruments of a destiny ordained from within.

(*The Person Reborn*, 123)

It is not a case of having a life with no difficulties, but of having the strength to surmount them. No one is exempt from conflict, which can strengthen a man as well as overwhelm him. There are physical combats with comrades who set upon us; moral conflicts with parents, with brothers and sisters, and with rivals; social conflicts; conflicts with oneself and with one's own failings. All of them are both useful in the reactions they arouse in us, and harmful in the cowardly defeats and proud victories to which they lead. Only the spirit which we bring to them determines whether they are good or evil.

We never find ideal conditions of life and work. We always think that if only things were different, we could really show what we were capable of. How many charitable movements there are which, in their penurious beginnings when ardent pioneers toiled in attics with packing cases for furniture, did wonders which they no longer accomplish now that they have become large and richly endowed organizations.

(*The Person Reborn*, 74f.)

The dignity of man derives neither from his strength nor from his weakness, in themselves, but from the use to which he puts them in God's service; that strength and weakness are merely natural facts, and are therefore neutral like everything else that comes from nature. They involve each its own dangers and privileges, its potential for good or evil.

(*The Strong and the Weak*, 171)

We are all in the habit of classifying people into two categories, the strong and the weak. There are those who seem doomed to be defeated and trampled upon. They have been so often beaten in this universal free-for-all that they are always expecting it to happen again, and this saps their strength. Those who know them also expect it, and gather strength and assurance for themselves from the fact. Even a stranger has an immediate intuition of their weakness, and treats them either condescendingly or aggressively – to do either is to humiliate them. On the other hand, the same intuition warns him of the strength of the strong, so that he adopts towards them an attitude of timidity or deference which confirms their strength. *Audaces fortuna juvat*, as the Ancients used to say.

In reality, the facts are more complex: we are all weak towards some and strong towards others. A man who at the office is constantly humiliated by an unjust superior may take his revenge at home by bullying his wife and children. And the superior is perhaps avenging himself in the office for the tyranny exercised over him by his wife at home. In the office the subordinate is paralysed in his defence by the fear of dismissal, and this feeling that he is a coward, sacrificing the justice of his cause to material interest, increases his humiliation, adding to it an element of self-contempt. This in turn increases his irascibility at home. But no one tyrannizes those around them without suffering remorse as a result, and this very feeling of remorse, repressed more often than not, aggravates still further his ill-temper.

(*The Strong and the Weak*, 18f.)

Each of us uses the weapons which he has at hand. For one it is physical strength, while for another it is precisely his weakness, a kind of extortion through appeal to his weakness, to the other's sensitivity, to despair. Many neuroses and illnesses, more or less consciously cultivated, serve as weapons by which things otherwise unobtainable are brought within reach. Impulsiveness serves one, while tenacious obstruction serves another; interminable or eloquent speeches win for some, while others use an obstinate silence.

(*To Resist or to Surrender*, 20)

The great human problem is not that of weakness, but that of strength. It is, in fact, that man feels in himself the mysterious power which God gave him when he gave him his dominion over nature. It is that he feels himself free to use it and to abuse it. It is of the strength and that liberty that man is afraid. That is why his fear grows with his strength. This is clearly seen in the case of the atomic bomb. It is evident, therefore, that the psychological salvation which consists in becoming as strong and as free as possible, contains in itself a dangerous weakness. There lies the vast difference between the Freudian doctrine of aggressiveness and Christian doctrine.

(*The Strong and the Weak*, 237)

The man who is incapable of sublimating his instinct of power, who clings to his post, who is unwilling to surrender anything of his prerogatives or his authority because he thinks in this way to prolong his youth – he is the one who ages morally.

(*Learning to Grow Old*, 203)

The strong have learned how to play their hand so as to win in the game of life, and they become prisoners of the game.

If we are to be strong we must also simplify life, shutting our eyes to its disturbing complexity. Thus the strong quickly become the prisoners of a systematizing habit of mind and a simplistic philosophy which ends by drying them up and cutting them off from true life.

Their repeated success soon leads them to believe that they are better than other people – above all, better than the weak, who think that God disapproves of them. Their success, even when it is unjust, they easily take to be a flattering sign of divine blessing; and this deprives them of the most fruitful experience this world affords, namely the experience of God's grace, to which the only road is repentance. I could cite here a great number of my patients who, after years of happiness and success, have nevertheless lived to bless the day when some affliction has allowed them to find a living *faith*.

(*The Strong and the Weak*, 169f.)

It is not always the strong who win, as the realists imagine. Nor is it always those whose argument is the most reasonable, as idealists would think. It is a well-known fact that little dogs bark much more than big ones, and sometimes scare them off by sheer noise. The strong can afford to give in majestically, for they have no need of victory in order to gain prestige; the weak become desperately obstinate in order to reassure themselves. They will argue against plain logic and even against their interests, because they cannot stand being defeated.

(*To Resist or to Surrender*, 13)

When the weak, who never retaliate, and appear content to allow themselves to be trampled upon, come to us and open their hearts, we find there an immense accumulation of grievances encumbering and poisoning them. It is only with difficulty that they bring themselves to put these things into words. They are afraid that we too will rebuke them for keeping this secret account of all the injuries, affronts and prohibitions they have suffered. They fear that we shall call them selfish and vindictive, and think them too critical of their parents, their teachers, their friends, and their husbands or wives.

The truth is that they are no more vindictive than anybody else. All they have done is to repress the natural reflexes of defence which come into play quite normally whenever a person is injured. Every attempt at domination of any living being arouses at once a legitimate movement of defence. In man a further movement, inspired by grace, may enable him to forgive. But this real forgiveness, always difficult, always miraculous, always productive of good, is one thing, whereas the premature suppression of the first movement of legitimate defence is quite another. Genuine forgiveness is a spiritual victory which frees the heart of all resentment. Suppression is but a weak reaction, liquidating nothing, and laying up in the heart a store of fierce grievances.

(*The Strong and the Weak*, 185f.)

The truth is that human beings are much more alike than they think. What is different is the external mask, sparkling or disagreeable, their outward reaction, strong or weak. These appearances, however, hide an identical inner personality. The external mask, the outward reaction, deceive everybody, the strong as well as the weak. All men, in fact, are weak. All are weak because all are afraid. They are all afraid of being trampled underfoot. They are all afraid of their inner weakness being discovered. They all have secret faults; they all have a bad conscience on account of certain acts which they would like to keep covered up. They are all afraid of other men and of God, of themselves, of life and of death.

Even the most gifted, even those who claim to be surest of themselves, have a vague feeling that their reputation does not correspond to reality, and they are fearful of the fact being observed. The most learned professor is afraid of being questioned on something he does not know. The most brilliant psychologist is afraid of being found to be the slave of some commonplace complex. The most eloquent theologian is afraid that the doubts that still haunt him will be guessed at. All know that their close acquaintances have discovered in their private lives failings which have escaped their crowds of admirers. All feel the mystery of life to be much deeper than they make out, and that what tomorrow has in store may suddenly reveal their weakness. What distinguishes men from each other is not their inner nature, but the way in which they react to this common distress.

(*The Strong and the Weak*, 20f.)

Faith and doubt

He who claims never to have doubted does not know what faith is, for faith is forged through doubt.

(*The Person Reborn*, 106)

One never really solves any problem. One may have the impression that one is doing so, thanks to some passing state of grace, but such states never last. We think we have solved a problem one day only to find it still with us on the morrow. Faith does not make life easier. Believers have as many difficulties as sceptics. In fact they often find a failure harder to bear, just because they are now sceptical.

(*The Adventure of Living*, 146)

Although faith retains its humility and trepidation, it is nevertheless the source of the only enlightenment that never disappoints. Although the believer must grope his way forward, experiencing crises and turning back – wondering if he has faith or feeling himself broken by God – and setting off again, he also finds on this difficult road, despite all the apparent setbacks, realities that are notably more stable than the great systems that men invent. Philosophical and scientific theories have their day; one after another they pass into oblivion, for all their power of suggestion as a vogue. But the rock of the Christian faith remains over the centuries; and sincere seekers all come to the same experiences and the same convictions, whatever the formula or the route they adopt. 'Faith,' one scientist writes, 'is more unshakable than knowledge.' Any human suggestion may provoke moral victories and a euphoria that is very similar to the effect of faith. But they do not last. Faith knows itself to be weak and uncertain, and yet like the reed it will survive the storm better than the proud oak. It knows that in this world it can never penetrate all the unfathomable mysteries of God, and yet, however tiny the light it receives from him, this is the only light that can really show it the way. Faith alone brings true peace.

(*The Person Reborn*, 175f.)

Sickness and suffering

We sometimes hear talk of a 'Christian medicine'. For my part I do not believe there is a Christian medicine distinct from ordinary medicine. What the Bible teaches us about nature and about man is true for the whole of medicine. Every sick person is faced with the problem of the meaning of things. Doctors, whether or not they are believers, can find real enlightenment on this subject only in the Bible. They will discover that all the men of whom the Bible speaks are, as it were, listening-in to God; that it is in that perspective that they view everything that happens to them. 'What is God saying to me through this?' is their constant question. That is the meaning of things. It is to ask myself what God is saying through that star that I am looking at, through this friend who is speaking to me, through this difficulty which is holding me up or through this trouble which befalls me. Once awake to this way of thinking, one discovers the true savour of life. Everything becomes throbbing with interest.

(*A Doctor's Casebook*, 35f.)

Our organs actually work much better when we leave them to their automatic functioning and do not think about them. That this is so is clearly shown in the case of the hypochondriac, who suffers from all kinds of functional disorders simply because his mind occupies itself with his body. These disorders attract the attention of his mind, and thus he is caught in a vicious circle. His preoccupation with himself develops in its turn into an automatism so powerful that he reaches a stage at which he is incapable of thinking of anything but his own ills.

(*The Meaning of Persons*, 96f.)

There are two extreme and opposite positions, whose ultimate source is to be found in our conception of nature. One view scorns nature, the other over-estimates it; one boldly opposes and coerces it, the other slavishly submits to it; one prescribes innumerable medicaments, the other none at all; one deprives men of the benefits of healthy living, and the other of those of medical science. We see, further, that these two views lead to a limitation of the fullness of human life and of human liberty. One makes men slaves of artificial and external processes from which they expect all help to come, and which they strive to multiply – think how many quite healthy people never go to sleep today without a sedative – and the other makes them slaves of their internal scruples.

(*A Doctor's Casebook*, 53)

The sick reveal to us the existence of universal problems with which those who are well manage somehow to come to terms, without finding real solutions to them. I always think of the sick as a sort of magnifying-glass which shows up an anxiety which we all have within us, more or less unconsciously.

(*A Place for You*, 33f.)

Modern man, despite appearances, is less aware of his own nature and motives, and is lonelier as he faces them. We pity the savage amid his mysterious, menacing spirits, but at least he shares his fears with all his tribe, and does not have to bear the awful spiritual solitude which is so striking among civilized people. And the primitive tribe does at least lay down a certain magical interpretation, which, however mistaken, is satisfying because it is unquestioned. In the same way, the modern fanatic, who unhesitatingly accepts all the dialectic and the slogans of his party, is happier than the sceptic. And this explains the strange resurgence of the primitive mentality which we are witnessing today.

Uncertainty is harder to bear than error. Now, science, by claiming to do away with the problems to which it has no answer, has left men alone in their grip. It leaves man in complete uncertainty as to the meaning of things, and the question still haunts him. That nothing should have meaning in this world is so contrary to that common sense which Descartes prized so highly, that man will simply refuse to believe it, in spite of all the theories of science. Men stricken by disease will never be prevented from asking whether their sickness has a meaning, and what that meaning is.

(*A Doctor's Casebook*, 104)

Job, in the midst of undeserved suffering, shouts to God, barraging him with countless 'Whys?' The book ends without God ever having answered. Thus the problem of unjust suffering has remained unresolved all through these centuries, that is, in its form of a syllogism over which all logical minds stumble: either God is all-powerful and therefore unjust, or else he is just but not all-powerful. Job, however, received his answer – an altogether different kind. It was not an intellectual reply, but an experience of God, once he paid attention to the questions God was asking. The philosophical problem of unjust suffering remains unsolved, but Job's attitude completely altered because he met God: 'I had heard of thee by the hearing of the ear, but now my eye sees thee' (Job 42.5). As long as men remain in a strictly intellectual frame of mind, they will always brandish their problems as so many challenges to which no satisfactory answer has come.

(*To Resist or to Surrender*, 58)

Strange though it seems, people become used to suffering, even though they may rebel against it. Some experience an odd feeling of depression just at the point where difficulties from which they have suffered cruelly are resolved. It is as if they could no longer do without suffering, or as if they found themselves weak, because their strength depended on reaction against suffering. After a long period of rain we find difficulty in believing that we shall ever see blue sky again, however much we may long for it. The same applies to the meteorology of the soul.

(*The Meaning of Persons*, 52)

The suffering of man is also the suffering of God. That is always my reply to those who tell me that they can't believe in God in the face of all the suffering that goes on in the world. God is the greatest sufferer; the state of the world causes him so much suffering that we are told that 'it repented the Lord that he had made man on the earth, and it grieved him at his heart' (Genesis 6.6). Throughout the Bible evil and death are the enemies of God; 'the devil', we read, 'that had the power of death' (Hebrews 2.14), a power hostile to God, which he will annihilate in the end: 'Death and Hades were cast into the lake of fire. This is the second death, even the lake of fire' (Revelation 20.14) – that is to say, the death of death.

(*A Doctor's Casebook*, 167)

If evil has two aspects, grace has also two aspects. The Bible, in affirming that there is a link between human ills and human guilt, gives the same answer to both. The account of the healing of the paralytic by Christ is well known (Luke 5.17–26). Before healing him, our Lord said to him: 'Man, thy sins are forgiven thee.' At this the hostile bystanders began to murmur against him. Then he healed him: 'I say unto thee, arise, and take up thy couch, and go unto they house. And immediately he rose up before them.' This incident is often quoted in connection with the relationship between sin and disease as evidence that the forgiveness of sins is the condition of healing, or, what is still more serious, as evidence that the sins of the paralytic were the cause of his paralysis. But Jesus did not say that at all. As he healed the sick man, he told his adversaries expressly that he was doing it in order to show them that he had 'power on earth to forgive sins', having asked them, 'Whether it is easier to say, Thy sins are forgiven theee; or to say, Arise and walk?'

It is quite clear from this account that Jesus is proclaiming his double power of forgiveness and healing, and that these two are bound up together. Throughout the Bible the healing of disease is presented as the symbol of God's grace which at the same time purifies the soul of its sin. Thus, while avoiding completely any suggestion of a causal link between the sins and the paralysis of the sick man, Jesus dealt at once with both.

(*A Doctor's Casebook*, 192)

The end of the road

I have sometimes made a distinction between the world of persons and the world of things, because human beings need to feel that they are loved personally, loved for themselves as persons, and because too often in our modern world they feel they are being treated as things, as tools of production. But the person is not pure spirit: it has a body which acts and feels; and man is one with his work; he reveals himself quite as much by his acts as by his ideas and emotions; and his ideas and emotions are but the inner echo of his encounter with the world through action. The person lives within the world of things, and gives it life. You cannot love people without loving things. I love sawing, filing, grinding, turning, nailing, glueing, soldering and cooking. And I love true dialogue, personal encounter, communion with my fellows. The same life-force drives us towards ideas, persons and things.

The important thing is the desire to do things, to understand and to know. To know people and science, and the diversity of human activities, drawing, painting and music, flower-culture and fruit-growing, and mechanical and electrical construction. Old age and retirement are a wonderful opportunity to widen one's field of knowledge and experience by undertaking things that one could not do when one had to concentrate on one's job. But the seed must be there already; this pleasure in learning and knowing must have been cultivated already throughout one's life.

And throughout one's life one can achieve growth through mixing intellectual and manual tasks. I get as much pleasure out of my workshop as out of my library, in my garden as in my consulting-room. But I think that there is more to this than personal taste. It is a matter of the deep springs on which one draws. Ploughing and sowing, milking, building, sewing and cooking have always been, along with his words and his smile, the primitive gestures by which man has manifested his humanity. In hunting, sex, suffering and feeling, he was not yet distinct from the animals. But the joy of being a man he experienced through these primitive gestures, long before he thought, before he thought that he was performing them, before he thought that he was thinking.

(*Learning to Grow Old*, 113f.)

Life is a movement, evolution, progression and not stagnation; it can be comprehended only in its incessant becoming, in its total continuity. You need a sense of history if you are to make sense of life. If you look only at the point where you are, you will see neither where you came from nor where you are going. One of the dimensions of your consciousness as a living being is missing if you do not enter into relationship with all age-groups, and more particularly with those who are nearing the end of their lives.

(*Learning to Grow Old,* 74f.)

If an old man sees that you are really interested in his personal life, you will see a wonderful transformation take place in him. His eyes that seemed dull will light up with a new fire; his face will come alive with unexpected emotion. He felt that he had been thrown on the scrap-heap, and all at once he comes to life again, becomes a person once more. Just like the child, the old man needs to be spoken to and listened to in order to become a person, to become aware of himself, to live and grow. You will have brought about something that no social service can ever do of itself: you will have promoted him to the rank of person.

(*Learning to Grow Old,* 72)

People talk of an age when we are exempt from passion. But the absence of passion really means anticipated death. If the frown of anger is no more, then the smile of pleasure will have gone as well; if there is no more indignation, neither will there be forgiveness; if there is no more anxiety, there will be no more hope either. That will come, alas, in the last extremity of old age, of course. But then it is not the triumph of wisdom, but rather decay. There is no further problem. There is nothing but a patient whose suffering the doctor tries to mitigate, and whose life he endeavours to prolong, and one never knows what is going on below the surface in the life of a human being, behind the appearance.

(*Learning to Grow Old*, 131)

The problem of old age does not concern only the old. It calls in question the whole of our society, and exposes its faults. That it is inhuman is verifiable at any age. But this is felt more especially in childhood, when we begin to discover the world and its injustices, and when we are too weak to defend ourselves. Later on, in the full strength of active life, we can at least fight, stand up to injustice, contend with fate. But when old age comes, we find ourselves powerless once again, and feel once more the pain of the faults in our civilization.

(*Learning to Grow Old*, 36)

I know nothing about what form life will take in the beyond, but I know that it will not be an unincarnate, abstract, impersonal world of ideas, of pure anonymous spirits or of phantoms. I know that I shall retain my personal identity; and it is a fact here below, in personal fellowship, in the person-to-person relationship when it is true, that I find a foretaste of heaven.

(*Learning to Grow Old*, 237)

Acknowledgments

All the books by Paul Tournier from which the extracts in this *Companion* have been taken are published by SCM Press. Dates of publication are as follows.

The Adventure of Living, 1966
A Doctor's Casebook in the Light of the Bible, 1954
Escape from Loneliness, 1962
Learning to Grow Old, 1972
The Meaning of Gifts, 1964
The Meaning of Persons, 1967
The Person Reborn, 1967
A Place for You, 1968
To Resist or to Surrender?, 1965
Secrets, 1965
The Strong and the Weak, 1963
What's in a Name?, 1975